THE WORLD

AT YOUR FEET

T I M   H A R T L E Y

THE
WORLD
AT YOUR FEET

IN SEARCH OF
THE SOUL OF FOOTBALL

First published by Pitch Publishing, 2021

Pitch Publishing
A2 Yeoman Gate
Yeoman Way
Worthing
Sussex
BN13 3QZ
www.pitchpublishing.co.uk
info@pitchpublishing.co.uk

A CIP catalogue record is available for this book
from the British Library.

ISBN 978 1 78531 794 1

Typesetting and origination by Pitch Publishing
Printed and bound in India by Replika Press Pvt. Ltd.

Contents

To Kevin
Happy now?

About the author

Tim Hartley loves and loathes football probably in equal measure. Despite decades of wandering, his obsession with the cultural, political and social relevance of our national game is undiminished. It seems the more bizarre the connection with football the better it is for him. Hartley is a journalist and broadcaster, a former vice-chair of Supporters Direct, chair of the Cardiff City Supporters' Trust and a director of the Welsh Football Trust. He is the author of *Kicking off in North Korea – Football and Friendship in Foreign Lands* (Y Lolfa, 2016), edited *Merci Cymru* (Y Lolfa, 2016) and has recounted his search for the soul of the game on the BBC's *From Our Own Correspondent* programme and in newspapers, magazines and websites. Hartley lives in Cardiff with his wife Helen, a fellow Cardiff City fan. They lost their son, Chester, to Partizan Belgrade some time ago.

Introduction

FIRSTLY, I wish I'd written this book. Not only is it utterly brilliant but there are so many moments in here where I found myself agreeing and saying out loud, 'I was at that game, too, and that's exactly what I thought.'

My first football memory was of the orange shirts of the famous Dutch team at the 1974 World Cup Final. My first Welsh football memory was losing on a chaotic day to Yugoslavia in the quarter-finals of the 1976 European Championships. It was probably the most perfect baptism for a Welsh football fan imaginable. We lost, we didn't qualify, we were on the bad end of some awful refereeing and there was trouble in the crowd. That match beautifully encapsulated in one afternoon what was in store for me and thousands of other fans in the decades that followed.

I love football. When I say these words in my own accent (now remember I'm from Merthyr Tydfil and have an almost clichéd, Gladys Pugh *Hi-de-Hi!* way of talking), people who aren't from Wales say, 'Oh, I thought you'd be a rugby man.' I am not. I mean, I always want Wales to win at rugby just like I would want my country to win even if it were at tiddlywinks. But football is my game. There are thousands in Wales like me and we finally had our glorious moment in the sun in France at Euro 2016.

Tim is the living embodiment of my kind of footballing Welshman. He's been there, seen it and done it with Wales. He is easily one of our most well-known, and liked, fans. He's played for the supporters' team across Europe and done stuff for charity in the name of Welsh football which makes me wonder what I've been doing with my life. He is Wales.

In this book, Tim bares his soul about the game he loves, and it's a wondrous thing. He takes us on a footballing tour around the world. But his experiences and reactions are always rooted in, and tempered by, his beloved homeland and its culture. He is part of a strange new tribe of football supporters that exploded on to the world stage in France with their good humour, colourful bucket hats and retro tops.

I knew this tribe existed before the Wales team met with any real success, but what fascinated me was that it had been allowed to slowly develop in its own petri dish. You see, ironically, by Wales never qualifying, this group of supporters became utterly unique. A whole culture arrived, fully formed and danced out from the wings of the stage of the Moulin Rouge can-canning down the streets of Paris singing, 'Don't take me home.'

I will never forget arriving in Lyon in the early hours after driving from rainy, dull Lille. As we checked in to the hotel the receptionist told me and my mate that he had stayed up to meet the 'Gallois' fans. He'd clocked our names, Owen and Davies, and wanted to tell us that he thought we were the best fans in the world. I genuinely thought I was going to be woken up from my month-long French dream at that point. We'd just beaten the tournament favourites, Belgium, and now this. Me and my butty, as we call our friends in South Wales, laughed at the ridiculousness of it all.

In this book, Tim tells you exactly where we all came from – because he lived it too. He patently adores his hometown club Cardiff City, and his homeland, but he loves the game itself as much and, in some ways, even more. He takes us to Germany and wonders what reunification actually meant for football in the east of that divided country. You can feel his melancholy on the day he watches the European Cup Final in a shut-down, Covid-conscious Berlin.

There are adventures in Hong Kong where singing the wrong song can land you in jail. Talking of jail, he goes inside one himself to meet a team of serving prisoners and learns how the simple act of playing with ten other human beings raises the human spirit, giving hope to some of the most needy among us.

I always hoped Wales would get to a major international tournament. We used to sing with such gallows humour, 'We'll never qualify', that I didn't in my heart of hearts think we ever would. A loss in a European Championship play-off to Russia in the mid-2000s broke me. It was then that I resigned myself to following Wales mostly as a social event. If we didn't qualify then at least we knew we could party better than anyone. But then we did qualify and all this marvellous football culture poured forward. The dam burst open. Books were written, films were made. It was glorious; I loved it.

I also loved this book. I read it in two days. It's not just a book for Welsh football fans, although, my compatriots, you will love it too. It is for all football fans because it's the story of the game. Whether you're an ultra in Clapton, or play for the Ukraine supporters' team, your story is right here – because Tim's story is our story.

Jonny Owen

1

How It All Started

THE CHANTS grew louder, the crowd swayed as one and I lost my footing, tumbling down under a heap of young men in flares and tank tops. I avoided a Doc Marten boot and struggled back to my feet with as much self-respect as I could muster. 'Yeah. Nothin' mate,' I mumbled, not that anyone was listening. For this was 1976. It was a week after my 16th birthday and I was a lone 'lad' on Cardiff City's Grange End terrace but this time supporting my national team. No dad beside me, certainly no mum in those days. Just me. And boy was I petrified.

This was no normal game. It was Wales v Yugoslavia and at stake was a place in the semi-final of the European Championships. We had lost the first leg 2-0 in Zagreb but our hopes were high. In terms of tangible success over the years, let's just say that the footballing gods had not been kind to Wales. Getting this far, reaching the last eight of the Euros, seems to have been almost airbrushed from our nation's sporting history. Before me that day, though, were some of the best Welsh players of their generation: John

Toshack, Terry Yorath and Leighton James. I don't think we realised how good this class of '76 was until well after the event.

The atmosphere inside Cardiff's Ninian Park was intense that afternoon; 30,000 fans packed the ancient, battered but oh so real football ground. It was also, sadly, the golden age of football hooliganism where passion, alcohol and teen spirit could lead almost anywhere. Up until then I had been more of a rugby boy and, compared with the respectful atmosphere watching the Black and Blues at the Cardiff Arms Park, this was to be a jolting culture shock. Sure, I had been 'down the City' on a couple of occasions, but that was with Brett from Barry and his dad who had chaperoned us well before kick-off to the posh seats in the Grandstand. This, though, this was something else.

I will never forgive the powers that be for denying generations of supporters the visceral experience of watching a football game standing on a terrace in a traditional ground. I was mesmerised by the sights, sounds and smells of Ninian Park. The enormous floodlights stretched high into the late spring sky like *War of the Worlds* giants peering over the cavernous stands below.

Four or five times a year Ninian Park hosted Wales's international matches. Bob Marley played a gig there just two months after the Yugoslavia match and Pope John Paul II also graced the pitch in 1982. It was a stadium venue before they became a big deal. In normal times it was the home of Cardiff City FC. The dark and imposing Grange End was Cardiff's 'end', where their noisy and partisan fans stood. Over the years the boys had rubbed shoulders with the best of Britain. Liverpool had the Kop, Manchester

United the Stretford End. We had the Grange End, like a mighty cave behind the goal. Who knew what beasts lay within?

There was a special Boys' Enclosure at the very front of the terrace, which was separated by a small wall from the main enclosure behind. If you leant on the wall you were just inches from the pitch itself. You could hear the players shout at each other and smell the wintergreen. We stood on ascending rows of blackened railway sleepers. TV cameras sat on a precarious platform dangling above our heads. Years later, I was told by a cameraman how they would shin up the gantry well before kick-off dragging the ladder behind them, 'Because you never know.'

There was a strange open-fronted shed with a sign saying 'Radio Ninian' at the far corner of the ground to our left. I think this basic tannoy system under a corrugated roof fancied itself as a pirate station washed up on the shores of Lake Ninian. It announced the teams, the half-time scores, the results of the Golden Goal competition and played us in and out of the stadium with ska classics. Every time I hear 'Liquidator' by Harry J All Stars, with its tinny drums and organ melody, I am taken back to that terrace and my mind conjures up the smell of Brut aftershave and chips fried in old oil.

A horde of faceless souls occupied this vast end. Our end. The Grange End. Pensioners in weather-beaten flat caps shielded children at the front, shaven-headed monsters with giant boots and braces behind. My hair was long in those days but I wore the obligatory check shirt and tank top. In the darkness of the stands a thousand cigarettes flickered. No smoke-free zones then.

It may have been Wales not Cardiff today but the routine was much the same. I found a space halfway up but close enough to the front so that I could seek refuge in the Boys' Enclosure if needs be. Sixteen is a slightly awkward age isn't it? I could play the hard man with the Ely and Llanrumney boys if I liked. But I was still fresh-faced enough that I could appeal to a steward's or a copper's paternal nature if the going got tough. And the going was about to get tough. 'One, two, three, four, five. If you wanna stay alive. Keep off the Grange End!' The chant sounds rather puerile now. It was then too but it was also great fun.

Captain Terry Yorath and his team though were the real men that day. It may be the quality of the television pictures from that time but looking back it seems the players then lacked the finesse of today's stars, such as Gareth Bale and Aaron Ramsey. But they had something else. They got stuck in. Forget the modern game's fitness regimes, dieticians and statistical analysis, in 1976 it seemed all we needed was passion and the will to win.

Either way it went horribly wrong for Wales from the word go. Yugoslavia were awarded a controversial penalty. Bang; 3-0 down on aggregate. Wales fought back and scored a goal to give us a glimmer of hope. We won a penalty which Yorath agonisingly fluffed, and we saw two further goals by Toshack contentiously ruled out by the referee Rudi Glöckner. One was for offside, the other because the East German official deemed that a John Mahoney bicycle kick assist was dangerous play.

There was something fishy going on. Glöckner had refused to start the match until the East German flag was flown above Ninian Park. Was he now deliberately favouring a fellow 'communist' team? I am not sure geo-politics entered into it on the Grange End that day, but the Welsh crowd went berserk anyway. Beer bottles and cans rained down on the pitch and some fans tried to climb the perimeter fence to get at Herr Glöckner. The stewards and police struggled to contain the crowd. Glöckner stopped the game and threatened to abandon it altogether. If that had happened it would have been awarded to Yugoslavia anyway.

At the final whistle a linesman was speared by a corner post – all because Wales had drawn an international football match. Yes, the refereeing had been questionable, but throwing a corner flag at a linesman. Really? The fans' performance that day earned Wales a UEFA ban from playing in Cardiff. For me though it had been a baptism of fire. I loved every enthralling, foul-mouthed and scary minute of it.

But there is a sporting history lesson here too. Ask most football fans and they will say the only finals Wales ever qualified for were the World Cup in 1958 and the Euros in 2016. Not so. Under their new manager Mike Smith that class of '76 were also a great team. They had beaten Hungary, Austria and Luxembourg, and to top their qualifying group, only to lose over two legs to this lot, 'the Brazil of the Balkans'. This match was their European finals.

Smith is perhaps one of Wales's more underrated managers. He deserves a lot of credit not just for this tournament but for his overall record with the national team. In his two spells in charge he oversaw 40 games, winning 15, drawing 11 and losing 14. He also had some interesting motivational techniques. Apparently the night before a match he would stick life-sized photos of the opposition on the walls of the Welsh players' rooms so they could get to know them. 'Rather footballers than the Bay City Rollers,' as he allegedly put it.

Ah, the 1970s, the decade that gave us Chopper bikes, 10cc on the jukebox, *Seaside Special* on TV and scarves tied around your wrist. It was also the decade of the 'dirty' Leeds team, the rise of Liverpool FC, the Home Internationals and the start of the club v country argument. Then there was Wales's superb Admiral kit, red with vertical tramlines either side in yellow and green and the crest bang in the centre. They didn't make replica kits for us fans in those days. I now wear a latter-day cotton copy of this shirt to every Wales match.

Perhaps it was the format of the European tournament in those days (only the semis and the final were played in one country) but this Wales team have become the forgotten men of international football. We rightly laud the groups of 1958 and 2016, but not the heroes of '76. For many of the men who gave their all at Ninian Park that May afternoon, the lack of recognition still hurts. As the captain Terry Yorath says, 'To this day it annoys me … we actually reached the quarter-finals of the European Championship with no help from anyone.' I agree, but for me this match will never be forgotten and I am privileged to be able to say that 'I was there'.

In the 40-plus years since that Yugoslavia game I have wondered whether this was the moment I fell in love with football. I moved away from Cardiff and only watched the occasional match from the terraces (Arsenal, if you must know). However, I never forgot the shared elation of the crowd at Ninian Park as that Ian Evans goal went in, the anger when the penalty was not awarded, the sheer wildness of it all. Yes, I was only 16, but it sticks with you doesn't it?

Since then I have watched football at all levels and all over the world, lower leagues, cup finals and play-offs. Nothing though can compare with that Saturday in May 1976. Maybe I am chasing my lost youth and that first, never-to-be-repeated, football fix. What a journey it has been. Long may it continue.

2

One Game, Two Nations

IT WAS the weekend of the delayed 2020 Champions League Final, the pinnacle of the professional game in Europe. German giants Bayern Munich, with Thomas Müller and Robert Lewandowski, were taking on Paris Saint-Germain who had scoured the world and struck gold with Neymar Jr, Kylian Mbappé and Thiago Silva. My warm-up for the big game was a little less stellar. As the rain bounced off the grim but evocatively named Allee der Kosmonauten in East Berlin I caught the tram across the city to the Mommsenstadion where Tennis Borussia Berlin, TeBe for short, were taking on Chemie Leipzig in the fourth tier of the German game.

Thirty years after my first visit to the new, old capital city I wanted to see how the other half lived and whether the supposed economic miracle that was German reunification extended to the game of football. Being Bayern Munich is one thing, to be TeBe quite another. The team is named after the nearby tennis club and you walk through a glorious shaded wood to get to their stadium. TeBe have a loyal fanbase but have only really flirted with success, appearing in the Bundesliga for just a handful of seasons. Chemie, too, have been through the mill with mergers, bankruptcy and demotion. Their real rivals are the once mighty Lokomotive Leipzig but they also live in the shadow of RB Leipzig – and all three come from the east.

When the Berlin Wall fell on 9 November 1989, East Germans looked forward to all sorts of tantalising western possibilities such as consumer goods and a free press, and there was now the possibility of travel, first across the wall and then to who knows where. Football would be no different, would it? Surely the fall of communism would mean new sponsors and investment, TV money and derby matches with the likes of German football's big boys, Bayern, Stuttgart and Bremen? East German marks could be traded for West German notes at a rate of one to one, pension plans could be transferred to the west. Millions of people thought they had become rich overnight.

It's difficult to think of living in a country where simple things we take for granted were either not available or so expensive that few people could afford them. The economist Rüdiger Frank said the symbol of the anti-communist revolution should have been a banana. It had been a luxury item in the east but could now be bought, at a price, on the open market. The banana was an exotic fruit; it suggested world travel and symbolised consumerism.

When unification officially happened, exactly one year after the wall came down, I walked down the Unter den Linden and drank vodka with complete strangers in the shadow of the Reichstag at the all-night party. It was a time of hope, of joy. But then came the hangover. In reality, unification also meant economic dislocation. Factories in the east closed and unemployment grew. Wages were roughly half those in the west whatever currency you were paid in. Economic output dropped and by 1991 four million people had relocated to the west – including some of their best footballers.

For my east-west match 30 years on, Chemie had been offered 150 tickets for this socially distanced Covid affair. The club couldn't agree on how to distribute them so they decided not to take up their allocation. That did not deter more than 200 fans who, like me, simply bought home tickets online. Yvonne Siemon lives in Leipzig and works in customer service. A lifelong Chemie fan, she was 12 years old when the wall came down. 'The club was always for the working class,' she said. 'I can't remember that much before 1990, but I do remember at that time we always had no money.' Yvonne's dad, Burkhard, is 69 and worked as a lawyer in Leipzig before retiring. He played football from the age of nine. 'We wore nailed studs in those days, before the aluminium screw-in things,' he said. The highlight of following Chemie for him was winning the league. 'Erfurt, 10 May 1964,' he says without hesitation. 'We won the cup in '66 but after that things went a bit downhill for the club.' Growing up, Yvonne watched Chemie with her dad. Despite her club's poor form she says that the first united all-German team in 1991 made a big impression on her as a young football fan.

Uwe Rösler was also part of a Leipzig footballing family – and a professional footballing family. He played for East Germany, went on to become a Manchester City legend and then manager of Fortuna Düsseldorf. Rösler was 20 years old when the wall came down. His father, who was also a footballer, had been interrogated by Stasi agents who tried to get him to spy on his team-mates at FC Lokomotive. The loathed secret police feared they might be planning to defect to the west. In exchange for Rösler senior's cooperation, the Stasi allowed him to continue his career without interference.

Things were different for the son, Uwe, and back in the early 1990s anything seemed possible. Speaking to the German website DW.com, Rösler says, 'We watched our idols on TV for years, for decades and then we got to play against them.' Rösler had a difficult start in the first reunified season of German football. He struggled at Dynamo Dresden and then at Nuremberg. 'It was another level of football, another level of scrutiny, the media and contract to cope with. It was a society with elbows. You had to look out for yourself. In the east we were more, from a collective. We were ... more team.' Rösler made the big time at Manchester City and between 1994 and 1998 he scored 50 goals.

At the time of unification, Ulf Kirsten was in his mid-20s and playing for Dynamo Dresden. Following in the footsteps of Andreas Thom, the first player to go over to the other side, he moved to Bayer Leverkusen. He said, 'It was new for us that a lot of agents and managers of clubs would turn up to matches or training sessions and that we would keep having them come up and talk to us. In the second half of the 1990 season, it really became a big thing with so many interested parties contacting us.'

Kristen immediately saw the differences in the approach to the game between east and west. 'We definitely trained a lot more in the east, twice a day,' he says. 'You actually never had a day off. In the Bundesliga, it was and still is usual just to do some jogging on the day after a match and then have the day after that off. That was uncharted territory for us.' More than 20 players left East Germany between 1989 and 1991 to sign for Bundesliga clubs, including future stars such as Thomas Doll, Matthias Sammer and of course the Leverkusen twin strikers Kirsten and Thom.

Steffen Freund was another early East German footballing export. He says the Stasi also tried to recruit him as an informer while he was at Stahl Brandenburg. In 1991 he joined the westward flow and was transferred to FC Schalke 04 where he established himself as an important midfield player. Freund says that in those early months of a reunified Germany, Bayer Leverkusen and other West German teams, came over with a few guys and bought the best players'. Rösler agrees, 'The Bundesliga clubs came over and hunted all the talent out of the east and the east clubs didn't really get paid the money they deserved to rebuild their clubs and their structure.'

For financial reasons, Schalke were forced to sell Freund in 1993 to Borussia Dortmund where he won the league twice and gained a Champions League medal. In December 1998 he transferred to Tottenham Hotspur where he won the League Cup, having already won the Euros as part of the united German team of 1996.

These stories of individual glory, however, are the exceptions and most teams in the east today are plodding along in the lower divisions. Not that any of this seemed to worry the Chemie or TeBe fans when I met them at the Mommsenstadion. German football at this level is a very different beast from the well-organised heights of the

Bundesliga proper. There was cheap beer on the terraces, an Antifa flag draped over the fence, no segregation and a delicious 1970s soundtrack rang out. 'Kids in America' segued into 'Ever Fallen in Love' and then into a great German cover of 'Blitzkrieg Bop' by Ramones. As I sang along to the chorus the guy next to me said, 'That's me.'

'Eh?' I mumbled through my face mask.

'That's me singing,' he said. 'It's called "Tebe Rockt!" It's "Blitzkrieg Bop" but in German of course.' And he laughed.

Denis Roters is a lifelong TeBe fan. He's got a full face, is slightly unshaven and wears his thick hair in a side parting across his forehead. He looks a bit like Jack Black in the film *School of Rock* which sort of suited the occasion. I bought him another Berliner Pilsner and we got chatting.

'Yeah. It's my band's cover version. We released it as a 7 inch vinyl to celebrate the club's 100th anniversary. It was on purple vinyl, the colours of our club.'

We talked about punk, football of course and inevitably politics. There is a little irony in the fact that TeBe is one of only two West Berlin clubs, both playing in nice middle-class areas, who are now fighting it out in this division with former eastern footballing powerhouses. Denis sees the unification of Germany as only now, 30 years on, really coming to fruition. He says, 'Things have normalised. Some parts of Saxony [former East Germany] are nicer than here. Really. You have a generation of supporters, citizens, who are too young to remember the past and that's probably a good thing.'

Denis was happy to talk and didn't seem too concerned about his team's performance. It was half-time, TeBe were 2-0 down and struggling to hold Chemie back. The 200 away fans moved as one green wall towards us. I was a little concerned but they just wanted to stand behind the goal in anticipation of seeing their team score. In the higher leagues of the professional game, 'changing ends' like this is just not allowed.

Yvonne Siemon says it's good to see her club finally coming out of the shadows. I asked her what was her favourite moment watching Chemie. 'Missing out on promotion in Schönberg, 2003,' she said. 'There were 4,500 fans away from home.' I was beginning to wonder if there was an inverted snobbery at this level of the game. The most memorable games are defeats. Not 'succeeding', so long as you stick together and suffer defeat as one, is a bigger badge of honour than winning and moving up the leagues. I knew the feeling.

Maybe for fans like Yvonne it's an acceptance of reality, the reality that, in terms of football, reunification failed. The dream of a new, unified and glorious all-German football community became a nightmare. When the time came the east wasn't really allowed to compete in a free market.

All the clubs in the Oberliga (East German league) were part of state-owned companies and the players were effectively paid by the state. When the wall came down the knowhow on marketing your club and drawing up contracts simply didn't exist. Eastern regional companies didn't have any money to properly fund teams and western sponsors didn't want to know. Investors at that time were interested in real estate not football.

Alan McDougall is a historian and author of *The People's Game*, which explores football in the former East Germany from 1949 to 1990. When the Oberliga was established, many 'bourgeois' clubs were disbanded and others renamed, merged and relocated. The teams that rose to the top had sponsors but in a communist society they were more like patrons and were usually part of a state-run industry or organisation. Dynamo Dresden and Berlin FC were related to the police, Lokomotive Halberstadt to the railway, Chemie Leipzig to the chemical industry. Motor Karl-Marx-Stadt was an automotive outfit and the postal service had its team, Post Neubrandenburg.

One team though rose above the others. Founded in 1966, BFC Dynamo were associated with the Stasi. They won ten consecutive league championships between 1979 and 1988. Argument rages to this day about how they did it. There were allegations that referees were bribed and bullied, and that the secret police could flex their muscles in the media and, not so subtly, poach players to join their team. Refs who wouldn't play ball didn't get to represent the German Democratic Republic in UEFA competitions. Foreign travel was then of course prestigious, valued and rare. There was genuine public anger at the favouritism shown to BFC and, in the mid-80s the SED, the ruling communist party, did secretly investigate the claims. It concluded that referees had given, by a margin of three to one, decisions in favour of Dynamo and a few referees were suspended for alleged bias.

McDougall says, 'If you talk to Dynamo fans they will tell you that there was never a smoking gun. There was no order to get referees to fix matches in favour of Dynamo. They had the most talented players, they had a very good youth talent scouting and promotion system, all of which was true and those were the reasons they emerge as the most dominant force in East German football.' He concludes that it was probably a bit of both but that Dynamo certainly benefited from some 'shoddy refereeing'.

Winning the domestic cup and the league of course meant European football. But the eastern clubs struggled in the forerunner of the European Cup. Like Celtic you might say, Dynamo were not being properly tested at home. On a week-to-week basis there was a lack of competition and once away from home everything was strictly controlled. As one commentator said of the East German team, 'Players were never free in the head.'

The West German businessman, Michael Kölmel, invested in many clubs out east. He saved Union Berlin from bankruptcy and also helped build what is now RB Leipzig. But even he saw that, for the game of football, unification wasn't going to work. He told DW.com, 'Many clubs made wrong decisions with the money. They didn't know what they were doing. They signed players and coaches from the west for way too much money.' How were they supposed to know how to run a professional football club when they had never had to before?

There were some success stories. Despite being smaller in terms of population than their neighbours, East Germany beat West Germany in the 1974 World Cup, the only time the two teams played each other. The single winning goal was scored by Jürgen Sparwasser. Ironically, in 1988 Sparwasser defected to the west while taking part in a veterans' tournament there. West Germany went on to win the trophy that year but the victory was celebrated on both sides of the Iron Curtain as a 'German' win. In 1989 Dynamo Dresden reached the semi-finals of the UEFA cup and the national team almost qualified for the 1990 World Cup. But in reality the East German national team were always going to be in the middle order of European football. Today not a single team that was part of East Germany's top division, the DDR-Oberliga, in 1989 is part of the Bundesliga. Dynamo Dresden almost went bust after a western German businessman took them over. He later went to prison for embezzlement. The last East German champions, Hansa Rostock, are in the third division.

You could argue that with Angela Merkel, the long-serving chancellor – whose family moved to live in East Germany – at the helm, easterners have fared quite well at the top of German society. But even now very few of the senior positions in politics, business, science, the media and, of course, football are filled by Germans from the east. This could be a result of the early westward post-communist brain drain in search of fresh opportunities.

The fusion of the East and West German leagues was also not fair. In 1991 the Bundesliga had 18 teams while the Oberliga comprised 14 teams. Instead of a genuine merger, all 18 western teams were retained and only two East German sides were allowed to join the Bundesliga. Six eastern teams were relegated to the second division and the rest sent from the first East German league to the third 'all-German' division including 1974 European Cup Winners' Cup winners 1. FC Magdeburg and record champions Dynamo Berlin.

Many say the changes made during unification put football in the east back at least ten years, though the game has many current heroes who hail from the 'wrong' side of that now imaginary border. The current youth development system, with schools and a scouting system from the age of ten, was devised by the East German Matthias Sammer. In 2006 he was appointed technical director of the German Football Association (DFB). Sammer was born and bred in Dresden. His 'all Germany' team had won Euro 1996 and he was named the tournament's best player. Sammer retired with a total of 74 international caps, 23 for East Germany and 51 for the unified side. Other famous players from the east include Michael Ballack from Karl-Marx-Stadt and the World Cup winner Toni Kroos, who came from the small city of Greifswald.

At the time of writing there are two 'eastern' teams in the Bundesliga. Union Berlin finally made it into the top flight, a genuine old East German outfit known as a dissenter's club. Then there is RB Leipzig. The rise of RB splits opinion. They were founded in 2009 by the energy drink company Red Bull, which bought the rights to a club in the fifth tier of football. Within seven years they were in the Bundesliga.

Traditional supporters like Yvonne Siemon say they merely bought their way to the top. Her father, Burkhard, is a little more forgiving. He says, 'I think they are an enrichment for the football in the east of Germany and the Bundesliga as they are playing good offensive football and it is fun to watch them.' He's not so keen, however, on their youth policy. 'With the abolishment of the under-23 team they have made a huge mistake in my opinion. Young players now have no further development options after the under-19 set-up.'

The differing fortunes of these two eastern clubs, Chemie and RB, reflect the way football has changed since Germany was reunified. Yvonne is in no doubt. 'Some people watch

RB because they want to watch "real" football. If you love Chemie you cannot like them as there are two different approaches. The Bundesliga is just about money making, the Regionalliga [where Chemie play] is for football romantics.'

I turned my attention back to the pitch at the Mommsenstadion. TeBe had managed to claw one back but the revival didn't last long. Morgan Fassbender rounded the keeper for a second time and it finished 3-1 to Chemie. Ah well. As we were about to leave I asked Denis Roters about the big match the next night, the Champions League Final. Would he, could he, support his fellow countrymen Bayern Munich? 'D'you know,' he said. 'I don't care. I really don't care who wins. I'll probably end up watching the ice hockey.'

I watched the final, socially distanced of course, in a bar off the Frankfurter Allee. In a dire game, Bayern Munich won the Champions League by beating PSG 1-0. I wish I had followed Denis's advice and watched the ice hockey.

3

Football Without Fans, Anyone?

I HAD a dream one night. Or was it a nightmare? The whole world had been attacked by some sort of deadly virus. Everything was on hold. There was no one in the office and nobody on the streets. The shops were closed; everyone went around wearing face masks. Then one business, only one, was allowed to flout the rules. Because of its money and undoubted influence, professional football was allowed to go back to work early.

'We can test everyone,' it said. 'We can all isolate in posh hotels. We'll be all right.' And besides, think of the money there was to be made from all those games on TV without having to bother with those troublesome fans. A win for everyone involved I think you'll agree.

But what was it like to actually be at a game without fans during the first Covid lockdown? Having watched the early behind-closed-doors matches on TV I was itching to know what, if any, atmosphere there was inside the stadium itself. Who would actually be there? And how would you react when your team scored?

So I jumped at the opportunity to cover the last scheduled game of the 2020/21 season at the Cardiff City Stadium for an American sport website. And it was a biggie. Just one point would mean my beloved Bluebirds flew into the Championship play-off semi-finals, destination the Premier League. The opponents Hull City, stuck at the bottom of the second tier, were staring relegation in the face. Following the enforced Covid break, for we Bluebirds, the longest season on record was about to become even longer.

Delighted as I was to at last see my team play for real, it was all a slightly unnerving experience. This was the first time I had ever parked at the ground on a matchday. There were no crowds to negotiate and I did feel rather grand driving through the barrier and parking smack bang outside reception. Stewards who I thought I recognised behind their face masks shepherded me to a distant entrance. My temperature was probed with one of those plastic handguns. I was asked to fill in a medical questionnaire before being given my pass and shown to my seat, which was clearly marked with yellow tape.

There were some 20 of us media bods scattered across the press box and a stretch of the main stand. The silent pre-match build-up was broken every so often as the radio reporters piped up, speaking animatedly into their microphones for a few seconds. And then there was silence as we all looked down at our iPads or notebooks. I peered over the pitch longingly at my usual seat in the Ninian Stand, empty and sad under the dying summer light.

The tannoy blared away, the same bland pop as ever, only the volume tonight was not as high as usual. As the teams entered the stadium they played Cardiff's unofficial pre-match anthem, the rousing war cry 'Men of Harlech'. We all usually sing it in something approaching unison. But today the words were not flashed across the electronic advertising hoardings and, in place of 20,000 people joining in, only the odd security guard clapped as we all usually did at the end of each line – a tinkling of support from hollow pockets around the ground.

The announcer went through both line-ups as he always does but there was no applause for our heroes, no jeers for the opposition. It seemed a bit odd: who was he talking to? He even offered his normal last-gasp encouragement, shouting 'Cardiff City – the Bluebirds' with his voice crescendoing to an expectant high. And once again – silence. Then came the referee's whistle and kick-off.

As the game got under way I was unsure whether fake 'atmosphere' was to be pumped into the ground. Some clubs do this to try to replicate the sound of a full house. Others, and Cardiff was one of them, left us to paint our own aural pictures. I asked Laurence, a journalist colleague of mine, what he thought of it all. He had covered quite a few matches during lockdown and he could still not get used to it. Laurence told me that at one club he had visited they had a range of sound effects on standby. The audio person hit the button sending out a massive cheer across the stadium for a goal – just as the ball was cleared off the line. As they say, 'You had one job.'

Cardiff needed only a draw to seal their position in the top six but they showed a hunger to win from the very start. The team played with real confidence and for once I knew it was only a matter of time before they would score. And so it proved. Junior Hoilett chested the ball down before smashing it into the bottom corner. Cue a few echoing handclaps and maybe a fist pump from the bench. It never entered my head to jump up and shout. Call it normative behaviour among the journalistic few, but I just wrote down Junior's name, the details of the move and the goal time.

Hull should have had a penalty but nothing was given. Their manager remonstrated with the fourth official but in the absence of any vocal support from elsewhere in the ground he seemed to calm down more quickly than is usually the case. And then it was back to business. Both sides had good chances but Cardiff broke away again and following a corner our captain Sean Morrison made it 2-0 with a firm header. Leading 2-0 in the first half! In normal time, we would have been going berserk. Again, though, I nodded knowingly and diligently marked my notepad.

Watching games on TV at home during the lockdown, we had switched streams to get the commentary plus the crowd sound effects. It seemed so much more real with the commentators having to speak over the unreal electronic fans. When Cardiff were not on Sky or the BBC we would watch the game courtesy of the club and the Football League's own streaming service.

At first we were dismissive of the media team's attempts to ape John Motson et al. The commentary was not polished, not the kind of thing you had come to expect over the years. After a couple of matches though you listened to the incisiveness of what they had to say. These two guys understood football the way we did. They too were fans but they also had something that we didn't have – knowledge. Formations and positional changes were dissected along with the usual naming of players and description of the bleeding obvious. They may have been 'amateurs' but their refreshing approach to the job offered so much more. I was left wondering why the mainstream media all seem to have adopted the same bland style of commentary. Professionalism? Maybe, but it's as if there is a fear of showing any spontaneity or individuality on air.

At half-time I turned to the guy sitting next to me, well three seats away actually. He was a scout from Fulham. 'Are you watching anyone in particular?' I asked. 'Not really,' he said and turned back to his notebook. The pages on his pad had goals and pitch markings printed on them whereas mine just had lines. I was a bit jealous. He told me that his club had sent someone to watch all three of the Cottagers' potential opponents in the play-offs. They had spies at Swansea and Nottingham Forest as well as having him here at Cardiff. As it turned out he was at the right match. Cardiff would face Fulham in the semis.

The disadvantages of playing in an empty stadium extend beyond the loss of atmosphere and revenue for clubs. Having no fans also removes the so-called 'home advantage', whereby statistically a team does better when playing at home. Referees are only human and a noisy home crowd can influence the decisions the officials make on fouls, yellow cards and the like. They will also allow less added time when the home team is winning but more minutes when they are losing, thereby giving the home team an extended opportunity to at least draw the game. A study of European football has shown that without fans any 'home' advantage is all but wiped out. The academic network The Conversation showed that home teams win only 36 per cent of the time when the stadium is empty.

The away team wins 34 per cent of the time. There really is very little difference.

I have some vague memory of an experiment which tested the saliva of players from both teams before matches. It indicated that there was more testosterone present in the home team's bodies thus giving them a small extra physical lift. A very basic 'defend our home' emotional response apparently brought about genuine physiological changes in players. I like this theory but think it may also be macho pseudo-science I gleaned sometime in the 1970s.

The experienced manager Mick McCarthy had a novel take on the matter. 'I don't think it matters if you're home or away if I'm honest,' he said before Cardiff played Preston towards the end of the 2020/21 season. 'When you're away from home, you travel the day before and you're in game mode from Friday, in the hotel, you're wired for that game. Travelling might even have a bit of an advantage. You're on the bus and you're ready for the game, already thinking about it.'

As play resumed at the Cardiff City Stadium for my behind-closed-doors game so did the noise from the pitch and the touchlines. If the coaching staff shout and swear as much as this during a normal game then I must have been a little deaf for more than a quarter of a century. Maybe they thought that they could be heard by the referee in the otherwise quiet stadium. I do wonder though whether appealing for a foul a little less often might be more productive.

Hull started brightly in the second half. Mallik Wilks came close with a swivel and a volley to the bottom corner, only for the shot to be saved by the Cardiff City keeper.

Yes, the Tigers roared, but not for long. Cardiff made sure of the win in the 82nd minute. Bennett's free kick bounced off the keeper only for the substitute Danny Ward to follow up. There was going to be no way back for Hull but despite this absolute trouncing I did not feel any real emotion. Of course I was glad of the win and to be there to witness it but I was one step removed from it, oddly depersonalised.

I have tried to work out why fans are so important at matches. The 'buzz' we associate with supporting your team is more than just sitting together. It's the pre-match drink and the walk to the ground. Under the stand you nod to people you may or may not know because we are all in this together. It's the Werther's toffee handed down from the old man from Cwmbran who sits behind me. The crowd actually moves together as a play develops. Heads turn, some half stand, and then either flop back into their seats or jump for joy as the goal goes in. The postman from Maesteg who sits next to me shakes his leg nervously like a Jack Russell dog. The shakes increase in tune with the action. It used to annoy me but now I find it almost endearing. Of course the game itself is central to all this but it is not in itself the whole experience.

It used to be vital for me to be there for a match, to actually see my team, win, lose or draw. Family holidays were never booked until the new season's fixtures came out. Tickets for away games, particularly when our allocation was limited, were sold and traded for old favours and friendships. Back in the bad old days when Cardiff fans were banned from going to Swansea I managed to get to an away game using my reporter's badge. The Vetch Field was a cauldron of anti-Cardiff sentiment. That night I sat on my hands, literally, so that when we scored I would not jump up and cheer. I wanted to but I didn't. But that was 20-odd years ago.

For me, without supporters, there was no true passion in the ground that night against Hull. It was all so … professional. It may have been my status as a reporter but unlike my usual engaged and frenetic self I adopted the detached attitude of the neutral, and I hated it. I refused to cover any more games live, preferring to sit at home with Helen and John shouting at the stuttering stream on TV.

The Covid 'empty ground' season was not to be a short-lived phenomenon. Not even football's money masters were able to wholly ignore government health regulations. Social distancing and empty seats were here to stay. There was no guarantee we would all be watching live football any time soon. As if it were a normal year we Cardiff fans were asked to pay in advance for our season tickets. Until such time as we could return to our seats we would again be offered the live stream, which normally cost £10 per game. That price would be deducted from the sum we had already handed over to my club in lieu of tickets (those in the Premier League wouldn't even get that). For the clubs it would be business as usual only without the paying fans at the stadium, those same fans who would be paying anyway.

At the final whistle that July night, despite Cardiff having made it to the play-off semi-finals, there were no celebrations. There had been passion all right but it had all been on the pitch, with 22 professional players playing a professional game. To his credit the Cardiff manager Neil Harris commiserated with the Hull team as the players traipsed down the tunnel to League One. There was polite applause from the three important people in the directors' box and the media scribbled their own thoughts in that measured, unbiased way of theirs.

As for me, I filed my report, uploaded the pictures and trudged out into the night happy with the win but nervous for the play-offs. Had I enjoyed supporting my team in a crucial end-of-season match even in these bizarre circumstances? Sort of. I was glad to have witnessed a game behind closed doors but I am not sure I would do it again.

(Cardiff subsequently lost to Fulham in the semi-finals.)

4

Football With Some Fans, Anyone?

LOCKDOWN DRAGGED on and the ban on fans in grounds continued. It seemed ridiculous that you could sit in a clubhouse, near strangers, pint in hand and watch a game on TV but you could not walk round the corner into the ground itself to stand in a designated space two metres from the nearest human being in the open air.

I was not the only one missing my football. Some supporters found ingenious ways around the ban. In the lower leagues you can usually find a vantage point overlooking the pitch. Television cameras at Welsh Premier League games always pan to a couple of old guys or a family, usually with a dog in tow, looking down on the action from a hillock. Mel Evans, the father of Aberystwyth Town footballer Jonathan, took it a step further. Mel is a bus driver and he simply drove his double-decker 48 miles along country roads to Bala and parked it outside Maes Tegid. Father sat on the top deck with ten other Aberystwyth supporters to cheer on the Seasiders and they were rewarded by seeing his son score.

At the other end of the game, the Premier League, ever keen to switch back on a revenue stream, had trialled games with a limited number of supporters and 2,500 spectators saw Brighton play Chelsea in a friendly. The EFL, too, experimented with restricted numbers. Hungary, Poland and Germany had decided that you can safely watch your team in a properly controlled environment. Hopes were high in Britain and the government vowed that within weeks we would have games with 1,000 fans in attendance. It was a start. The virus though had other ideas. Covid FC made a dramatic second-half comeback and plans for a partial and staged return of fans from 1 October were suspended. Down came the shutters and it was back to a TV stream and fake crowd noise. So the onus fell back on me to find a way to support my team in a stadium.

Help came from an unlikely source. My son Chester was going to cover Wales's UEFA Nations League game in Bulgaria. It's a strange competition which promises all sorts of tenuous routes for qualification to proper international tournaments. I had been asked to cover it for my pals at Prost International but after my experience at Cardiff City I couldn't face sitting there again, alone, mute and pretending to be a neutral.

The Football Association of Wales may not have been selling tickets but Bulgaria were letting fans in. Whatever the Nations League is, this match would be a competitive fixture and I have not missed one with Wales, home or away, for longer than I can remember. Would supporting Wales with at least some supporters present be a different proposition from the Cardiff experience? Let's do it! One problem though – how do you get in? And that's where

Chester comes in. 'No problem,' he said. 'I've got a mate in Sofia. He'll sort you out for tickets from the Bulgarian end.' And he was as good as his word.

'Wales Away' has become quite a thing in our footballing circles. 'The best-kept secret in travel,' as one supporter told a television reporter some years ago. During the 1980s and 90s our national team were, well, not very good but the trips were always excellent. A key feature of Wales Away is that you have no choice over where you go. Not many people holiday in Azerbaijan but we have been there three times, because that's what the fixtures dictated. A few days travelling to Moldova? Yes please. And then there was a week in Nanning, China. The China Cup was a money-making exercise for the Football Association of Wales but a deliciously bizarre trip for us fans.

The Wales Away contingent happily share travel plans and advice on where to go and what to see. There is a pride bordering on a snobbery as to how many of these away games you have attended, when you started going and the strangest encounter or journey you have made. Some English fans, tired of the behaviour of a small but unpleasant minority of their own support, have opted to follow Wales and have been made welcome.

I should have known this Bulgaria jaunt would be no normal trip. Stansted Airport was deserted as Kevin and I sat down in the bar for a pre-flight Guinness. That emptiness of course may not have been due to the virus but the £6.20 price tag of the beer. Normally the bars would be heaving with Wales fans in their replica tops from down the years chatting animatedly about new players, our prospects in this competition and the likely cost of the beer in Sofia. There would have been red, white and yellow bucket hats aplenty, Welsh dragons draped over shoulders and old friends hailed across the bar. 'Was he that guy we met in Cyprus? Iceland?' 'No, he's the Wrexham fan we had a meal with in Slovakia, I think.' Part stag night, part family reunion, these trips are always friendly and good-natured. Not today. It was just Kevin and me in a dark and subdued airport bar in deepest Essex waiting to be called to our gate.

According to Chester's friend, there were 8,500 tickets on sale for this match at the Levski Stadium. There had been some confusion as to whether we were allowed to travel. Chester and I were fine because we were both working there although covering the game from different angles. He had managed to acquire five tickets but we lucky ones were a little restrained as we met up on Vitosha Boulevard, the tree-lined pedestrian street that runs through the middle of Sofia.

Leigh had flown in from Sweden where he now lives. Chester had driven up with his mate Marko from Belgrade. Perry had been in Greece and came over too. It was like the old days, only of course it was not. There were no flags dangled from the awnings of the city centre bars, no chants or songs to be heard. None of us was wearing a football top and we had no idea how we would be welcomed in the ground. Bulgarian football fans do not enjoy the best of reputations. We decided that we would try not to speak to each other in the ground and if Wales were to score, well, let's just say we weren't sure how we might react.

The conversation turned to the Wales Away phenomenon – best trips ever, longest journeys, most uncomfortable accommodation. The team's performance doesn't feature that much in these discussions. Over some strong coffee and even stronger rakija, someone mentioned that Tommie C had been honoured for having attended more than 100 Wales away games. Perry was the granddaddy of our little group that night but to be fair to him he stayed silent. I had to ask. 'Go on then, Perry, how many aways have you done?' 'Oh, 120 something. You lose count after a while,' he grinned.

In these Covid, locked-down and restricted times there was, however, a new question to be answered. Which Wales away match had witnessed the poorest away following? Could we be record-breakers tonight? The lowest number of travelling supporters of all time? It seemed strange that the holy grail of groundhoppers would be the game with the fewest of you there. Wales had played a friendly against Qatar in 2000. John Robinson scored the only goal in Doha. 'There were some 15 or 20 at that one,' said Perry, 'and no I was not there.' Oh dear. 'However,' he went on, 'I was at the match in Brasilia in 1997. It was arranged at very short notice and there were only eight Wales supporters there.' Game, set and match to Perry? There were five of us in Sofia so far, so let's see.

The city centre had been very calm and there was hardly anyone on the approach to the Levski Stadium. We had seat numbers on our tickets but were allowed to move freely around the ground. Chester took his seat in the press box opposite. Kevin, Marko and I considered our options. There were so many empty seats. We eventually sat, masked, on the halfway line, politely distanced from our fellow Wales fans. I mumbled the national anthem to myself so as not to stand out and the game kicked off. There is a running track around the playing area and with only one section under a roof, this bowl of a stadium seemed even more open and empty than what I had experienced at Cardiff.

There were a few Bulgarian supporters scattered in groups of threes and fours. The official attendance was said to be 1,000 but I think we counted some 250. We wondered if at €9.50 each the tickets were just too expensive for the average Bulgarian. In the hollow stadium it was again interesting to hear how much shouting goes on between the players and managers on the pitch, but this wasn't international football as we knew it. Kevin said what I think we had all been privately thinking, 'Of course it's great we got in. But it's a bit rubbishy really.' Marko laughed. 'You guys are so spoiled. I watch Partizan Belgrade week in week out. This would be a good crowd in the Serbian Super League.'

The Wales team had been depleted. Our talismanic players Aaron Ramsey and Gareth Bale were out and our striker Kieffer Moore was also unavailable having picked up two yellow cards. The Bulgarian team though were going through a very bad spell, with just one win in 18 competitive matches. Wales had the better of the play but Harry Wilson and Rabbi Matondo spurned goalscoring opportunities. The previous weekend we had played out a mind-numbingly boring 0-0 draw in Ireland. This performance by our young players was a step in the right direction but we really needed a goal. The average age of this team was just over 22. Whatever Ryan Giggs does for Wales he certainly does not rest on the laurels of the heroes of Euro 2016.

Kevin felt the team was disjointed, disorientated even. 'They're just going through the motions,' he said. 'I spend half my time at these games talking to friends and shouting at the officials. I can't do that. You know, the trip is the reason we come, the game is just the excuse. If only we could have a few hundred fans here. It would make all the difference.' There was the odd cheer but more often groan from the few Bulgarian fans around us who had made the effort to turn up, but their heart wasn't in it. We were still unsure as to whether we could come out as away supporters. From behind us we heard Leigh and Perry cheer. I turned round to see the steward put his finger to his lips to shush them up but there was no hint of anger.

Our keeper Wayne Hennessey went off injured in the 79th minute and I feared that despite an okay defensive performance Wales would be lucky to hold on for a draw. What do I know? Six minutes later Neco Williams crossed to Jonny Williams whose first-time shot went into the roof of the net. It was Jonny's first senior international goal. Brilliant. I couldn't help but let out a muffled shout. Leigh and Perry threw caution to the wind, and stood up and applauded. With just a few minutes left the steward this time winked and smiled at the apparently lone Welsh fans. I think he was saying, 'You deserve that for coming all this way.' At the final whistle the young team celebrated and came towards us to acknowledge our presence and support. We had collected ten points from 12 in our first four matches and were sitting on top of group four in League B. It's not often that Wales fans can say something like this, let alone, 'I was there.' But we were.

As we left the ground we met long-standing travelling fans Tim, Lucy and George. That made us eight Welsh supporters – a joint record low number of fans? Chester joined us and after a couple of drinks the atmosphere started feeling something akin to a normal away trip. We reviewed our strange circumstances in Bulgaria, how we got there, how we got our tickets and what it was all like. 'It was a bit weird wasn't it,' said Lucy, 'like being in church. Frightened to say anything in case you might upset someone.' Chester had loved the experience. 'We've got to see our national team with just a few of us real friends here. There have been no crowds, no hassle. I wish it was like this every time we play away,' he said. He had seen two more Wales fans sitting in front of the press box. When our goal went in they had sang out 'Bread of Heaven'. So, including Chester, there had in total been 11 of us away supporters. No record for low attendance then, but hey, it had been a privilege to have been there.

We walked home through a deserted city, moonlight dancing on the domes of Alexander Nevsky Cathedral and the minaret of the Banya Bashi mosque. The pandemic had cast a long, unsettling shadow over this unique away-day. Perry broke the silence. 'I felt safer in that stadium tonight than I do in Tescos in Cardiff Bay,' he said and we all nodded in agreement. It's amazing how a single goal can change the way you view a game. As in the Cardiff City Stadium it had been a strange footballing experience. Maybe it was the win or the shared effort of actually getting into the game, but this time, even in the company of just a handful of fellow supporters, it all seemed worthwhile.

5

Red Star Over Hong Kong

'HE'S NOT bad that Billy is he?' said my new football friend Joe. 'Pushes forward well for a centre-half.' The blue flag of Hong Kong Football Club fluttered in the sunshine above the Happy Valley racecourse, the home of HKFC. Next to it flew the red flag of China, a reminder, if it were necessary, that although it may be a 'Special Administrative Region', this former British colony is now very much part of the People's Republic.

The People's leader, Xi Jinping, had said so at the 19th communist party congress. In October 2017 more than 2,000 delegates had sat in the Great Hall of the People in Beijing and enshrined Xi's guiding ideology in the country's constitution. Alongside 'reform' and the 'socialist rule of law' there was to be an emphasis on the implementation of 'one country two systems' and the reunification of the motherland – a clear reference to nationalist Taiwan and of course Hong Kong.

Within days of his speech Mr Xi extended the law on disrespecting the national anthem to Hong Kong. Since the pro-democracy protests of 2014 football fans here had booed the Chinese anthem, 'March of the Volunteers', when Hong Kong played. The city state fields its own team in international competitions but had already been fined by football's world governing body FIFA for the fans' unruly behaviour.

Under the newly extended law those who do not show sufficient respect face up to three years in prison. I'd seen the story unfold in my guesthouse on local TV the previous night. Images of angry fans turning their backs on the anthem were shown over and over. Just as in the United States, where President Trump had criticised footballers who'd protested by kneeling during the playing of 'The Star-Spangled Banner', for China too the national anthem is a big deal. Some tried to play it down. Amid the headlines about lowering barriers to trade, continuous growth and innovation, the *South China Morning Post*'s Tony Cheung tried to allay the fans' fears. 'Refusing to stand will not mean arrest,' he wrote.

I'd gone to Happy Valley to see if the beautiful game was indeed a hotbed of anti-Beijing agitation. HKFC were playing Kwun Tong in the second tier of Hong Kong football. The teams themselves offered a bit of an insight into the region. The HKFC XI was made up of 'westerners', expats probably, English being the language on the pitch. Kwun Tong, meanwhile, were Chinese and the coach shouted from the sidelines in Cantonese. I wondered if this was a case of one game two systems within one country two systems.

Over a half-time pint of excellent Sportsmen's Pale Ale I spoke to the few supporters who were watching. 'They want to criminalise us for having an opinion,' said one man who didn't want to tell me his name. 'They're rolling back our freedoms,' said Joe, who had stood next to me during the first half. He wasn't that interested in politics to be fair, but then neither are a lot of the Brits living here. 'Look. It's a pro-democracy thing, yes, but as football fans we should really be asking why we don't have a team in the Chinese national league. There's big money there. And this lot,' Joe said, pointing at the players having their half-time drinks, 'why, we can't even pay them a decent wage.' A mixed bag of opinion then, hardly the stuff of revolution.

On the streets of the Special Region, life carried on as normal. In the glass and concrete palaces of Hong Kong Island, the banks and insurance companies were striking multimillion-dollar deals. In the markets of Kowloon anything and everything was being bought and sold. Hong Kong is like Manhattan on steroids. It and Shanghai, like so many Chinese cities, are massive economic engines, national cash cows. So why has President Xi chosen to pick this particular fight?

He could have been flexing his newfound political muscle, giving a gentle reminder to everyone who's really in charge. Beijing believes that Taiwan, Macau and Hong Kong are all Chinese. It says so in the constitution. The so-called Umbrella Revolution of 2014 may have appeared to wither away peacefully but the president and the communist party was not going to stand for any further public displays of discontent, least of all those shown on television across the world to a footballing audience of millions.

That visit to Hong Kong FC was in late 2017. I liked the idea of the protests and was proud that football supporters could enrage one of the most powerful men on earth simply by 'disrespecting' the national anthem. They say sport and politics should not mix but there are dozens of examples of where this has happened for good, and bad, in the game's history.

Football clubs can be associated with different religions or the politics of their supporters. FIFA is insistent that its constituent members be wholly independent of government. Countries all over the world, from Albania to Iran to Peru, have at different times been accused by the governing body of political interference in the running of their domestic game. Some have been suspended from the federation. But what of a political stance being taken by the fans themselves as in the case of Hong Kong? The authorities take a dim view of displays of racism and homophobia but I can't see them getting involved in the internal politics of individual countries.

We know that, within FIFA, votes for top positions and the awarding of tournaments to specific countries have been traded and bought. Corruption was, and maybe still is, rife. My own national team has a group called Wales Fans for Independence who before home games march from Cardiff city centre to the stadium at the edge of town under banners demanding independence from the UK. (The 'authorities' have remained silent on this – I guess their view is that whatever goes on outside the stadium stays outside the stadium). Whether it is with a small 'p' on the terrace or a big 'P' in the executive committee meetings, politics is all around us and it is in football too.

In that sense the Hong Kong anthem debacle looks like any other, albeit very particular, use of football for political ends. I thought that like the democratic 'umbrella' protests of 2014 it would prove to be a short-term and rather timid expression of annoyance at what was surely a fait accompli: Hong Kong belongs to China, even if its financial importance to Beijing meant that for decades it had been cut some slack on its more liberal ways of working and thinking. Surely it would all simmer down, the anthem law would never be implemented and Hong Kong would carry on making money for itself and for mother China. How wrong can you be?

In June 2019 the smouldering discontent in the Special Region erupted. A new law was to be introduced which would allow people charged with a criminal offence in Hong Kong to be extradited to the mainland. There they would be tried in wholly Chinese courts under Chinese law. The fear was that the city's judicial independence would be undermined and that the new powers would be misused to harass dissidents. Activists and journalists, indeed anyone who took a different view from the official line dictated from Beijing, would be unfairly targeted. 'You don't like the communist system? Wanna protest against our anthem and all things Chinese? Come this way. Across the border. No, we insist.'

After months of wrangling, Hong Kong's leader, Carrie Lam, agreed to suspend the extradition bill but it was a case of too little too late. The protesters were emboldened and widened their demands to include a call for full democracy. Clashes between police and activists became increasingly violent. The demonstrators stormed parliament. The island's airport was blockaded and hundreds of flights were cancelled.

The protests downtown became a regular weekend fixture. Fire bombs were thrown at police who responded with water cannons, rubber bullets and tear gas. There were injuries on both sides, scores of people were arrested, and some died. Reporting and internet restrictions meant that little of these protests was seen on the Chinese mainland but this is not what Beijing wants any part of the motherland to look like. After initially staying quiet it condemned the protests as 'behaviour that is close to terrorism'.

Undeterred by the threats, a new unofficial anthem for Hong Kong was written. 'Glory to Hong Kong' was unveiled by a group of musicians wearing goggles and gas masks aping the dress of the demonstrators. Following the booing of 'March of the Volunteers', it was first heard at Hong Kong's World Cup qualifying match against Iran and was subsequently sung at shopping malls around the city.

Here's a translation of the anthem from the Shanghaiist news website:

> For all of our tears on our land
> Do you feel the rage in our cries?
> Rise up and speak up! Our voice echoes
> Freedom shall shine upon us.
> For all of our fears that linger
> With faith, we shall never surrender
> With blood, tears, and sweat, we shall stride ahead
> For this glory, liberal land.
> When the stars no longer guide our path
> In the fog, the horn of conscience summons us.
> 'Preserve! For we are as one, with poise and be brave

Courage, wisdom are long with us.'
The dawn has come. Let's revive our Hong Kong.
Revolution of our time! For righteousness!
Democracy and liberty, wish them long last here
For the glory of Hong Kong.

Now how about this for a piece of timely football scheduling? In December 2019, China faced Hong Kong in an Asian qualifying match in the South Korean port city of Busan. Some 200 Hong Kong fans chanted and banged drums to drown out a tiny pocket of 'Chinese' supporters before kick-off and of course sang their new anthem. Avoiding any potential embarrassment, television coverage of the match back home in China did not show the anthem being played but cut in as the players were shaking hands.

Opinion on the terrace in Busan that night was divided. 'Football is important,' said Thomas Lam, who had flown into South Korea the night before the match. 'But this is a good time to show the world about what's happening in Hong Kong, too.' Cai Xudong, a Chinese student studying at Busan University, preferred to see the game solely as a sporting event. 'Football is football. Politics is politics,' he said.

China beat Hong Kong but what seemed at the time a bit of mischief by football supporters now has a grim, prophetic feel to it. Roll on six months and the inevitable happened. With ironic timing, on the 31st anniversary of the 1989 Tiananmen Square crackdown, Hong Kong's Legislative Assembly voted in favour of the National Anthem Bill. Now, anyone who shows disrespect to the 'March of the Volunteers' faces large fines and up to three years in prison.

The law also required that schoolchildren in the territory be taught the official anthem and its history.

At the same time the Chinese government agreed a comprehensive new security law that would see China installing its own security agencies in the city-state for the first time. On Tuesday, 1 July 2020 Hong Kong's new national security law, which targets secession, subversion and terrorism with punishments up to life in prison, came into effect. 'One country, two systems?' Not for much longer it seems. Looking back, singing a song you didn't really like might have been a small price to pay to retain the status quo you really did like.

6

Beautiful, Beautiful Chaos

CARS, BUSES and pick-up trucks with people hanging out of the windows and sunroofs rumbled through the night crowd. The sun had set hours ago but it was still hot. The heat and humidity wrapped you in a blanket of comfort. Waving flags and blowing plastic vuvuzela horns, the yellow-shirted supporters of Gabon wound their way from the Stade D'Amitie to Libreville city centre. The host country had just drawn against Cameroon, sending them out of the 2017 Africa Cup of Nations. Imagine what the party would have been like if they'd won?

We took a break from the long walk home and grabbed a bottle of Regab beer at a roadside bar, looking on at the kaleidoscopic procession. It was more of a shack than a bar, a couple of pieces of corrugated iron draped over some old planks offering a little cover for the plastic tables and chairs. A man in his 20s plonked his bottle down next to mine, rocking the rickety wooden table. Christian had studied politics and had worked in South Africa, Ethiopia and, he told me this more than once, in Dubai. 'I'm so glad you're here,' he said unprompted. 'It's a safe country this, really safe. You are most welcome. But the government. No, don't talk to me about them.'

I was a bit taken aback. I am usually loath to instigate such conversations in a new country. It's not really my place to do so. The object of Christian's anger was President Ali Bongo. He told us how Ali had taken over from his father Omar Bongo who had controlled Gabon for more than 40 years. There had been accusations of family embezzlement, human rights abuses and of irregularities during the 2016 presidential election. Gabon is oil-rich but a third of the population still lives in poverty. We'd been told to avoid political demonstrations, but just like the World Cup in Brazil, as soon as the tournament started the street protests stopped.

The Africa Cup of Nations is the continent's biggest football showcase and Gabon wanted to put its best face on for the world. But AFCON, as the competition is known, has also had its share of controversy. The 2015 hosts, Morocco, refused to hold it because of fears over Ebola and in 2010, in Angola, the Togo team bus was attacked by gunmen, killing three people. Before they had even left for Gabon, Zimbabwe's players revolted over money and accommodation while the tournament organisers faced a lawsuit over the sale of international television rights.

And then there was the spend on the venues themselves. After the Morocco-Ivory Coast match at the Stade D'Oyem, Chester and I had trudged through thick mud as we left the gleaming stadium. The approach roads hadn't been properly tarmacked. This arena in the jungle of northern Gabon looks like becoming a white elephant. It cost tens of millions of dollars to build, is far from the town and is expensive to get to. Would it ever be filled again after AFCON was over? Local people say the money could have been better spent. But Junior Binyam from the Confederation of African Football said just building the stadium itself had made an immediate impact, 'It's all about making water available and bringing electricity for the neighbours of the stadium.' From what we could see the nearest neighbours were miles away in the town itself.

So is the Africa Cup of Nations really a celebration of the beautiful game and a showcase of the best this continent has to offer, or just a vanity project for presidents and governments, reinforcing a western prejudice of self-indulgence and poor governance across the continent? And what about the fans?

Crowds are always small for AFCON finals and every two years the organisers say they will try harder next time to increase attendances. But some groups of fans can and do travel long distances to enjoy the tournament. The teams have lovely nicknames: the Stallions of Burkina Faso, the Elephants of Ivory Coast, the Indomitable Lions of Cameroon, not forgetting the Panthers of Gabon. However small they are in numbers, they provide a proud, colourful and noisy celebration of the game.

The tournament organisers had their own newspaper. *Esprit* was full of praise for Gabon's hospitality and it was not just hype. Chester and I walked the streets of Oyem for about half an hour in the midday sun, looking for a ticket for the Uganda versus Mali game. As had happened in Libreville, a knot of confident lads came over to us. They were asking ridiculous prices for tickets. They could get us the precious *billets*, but not just yet. 'This afternoon,' said the main man imploringly. 'Pay us now and we'll get them for you by this afternoon.' 'Nothing doing,' I said and we walked on. I feared we had come all this way for nothing. But then a young girl in a pressed school blouse and neat blue skirt gestured for me to follow her. She led me to a small office with little flags announcing 'billets ici', or 'tickets here', but the woman behind the counter said, 'No, not here. Try the stadium.'

Exasperated, we left the stuffy office but after a few words with strangers the girl pointed us towards a man in a well-pressed suit. 'Bien sur [of course],' he said, and produced two match tickets from his pocket. 'Combien [how much]?' I asked as I got my wallet out. We had expected the precious tickets to be expensive or for there to be a mark-up for foreigners but neither he nor the young girl would take a single Central African Franc for their generosity.

* * *

Our visit to AFCON offered so much more than the usual two weeks of football and cold beer in the sun. Gabon is definitely not a holiday destination; easyJet won't be flying there any time soon, but travelling across the country between games offered one of the most insightful journeys I have made, and it had little to do with football itself.

The road from Libreville to Oyem was long, winding and very, very slow. Cramped in the back of a Toyota minibus we stopped to pick someone up on the edge of town. 'No, too expensive,' she said to the driver and on we went. But not that far. After half an hour the bus needed a new air filter, so with all of us still on board our vehicle was pulled over and parked above a pit in a garage. The driver's seat was lifted up to provide access and down burrowed the mechanic. After much banging and swearing, 20 minutes later, all fixed up, off we went. But this time only as far as the pumps to fill up with diesel.

The driver had a wild beard and a short fuse. He was angry with something or someone and shouted constantly into his mobile phone. The back of his head was tinged with grey hair. It was unkempt, as if it was growing against his will. This was certainly no middle-aged fashion statement. We slowed down and stopped yet again. No one complained as we waited another ten minutes for the driver's rucksack to be passed through the window to him. We think he'd left it back at the garage. 'Enfin. En y va!' as they say in French, and off we went.

They were building a new road north out of the capital but like our journey the work was slow going. Weaving around potholes the width of the road itself, we banged and crashed our way through the ramshackle suburbs and into the green infinity. The bearded bad-tempered one inserted a CD into the dashboard and the bus boomed to the bubbling bassline of Afro beat. Layered on top were a mass of jingly guitar riffs. Are these west African rhythms wholly repetitive? Or do they change just a note or phrase every so often, almost imperceptibly? This sub-Saharan Philip Glass gave you a jolt when you picked up on a change in the otherwise uniform rhythm. The drum beats were complicated and I wondered how many members your band would need to play this kind of music.

The tune blurred in my head, becoming a hypnotic rhythm which took me over. Gradually the jerking discomfort of the road was blotted out, leaving just the acrid smell of human sweat in various stages of decay – the woman in front of me, so big that she took up almost a whole row on her own, the strange man next to Chester who for some reason was wearing a suit jacket in all this heat, and the aged, worn seats themselves. Damp, putrid wetness and human smells oozed from every inch of the Toyota. But I didn't care. The sun was shining and we were driving at breakneck speed through a quilt of leaves and vegetation.

I wondered if the music was a deliberate distraction from our privations, the dangers of the road and the bearded one's seeming death wish. You simply would not have allowed a taxi driver to do this at home. 'Okay pal, that's it. Enough,' you would have said. 'Stop the car. I'm out of here.' But we had six hours to go until Oyem and the sooner we got there the better. We swerved, bobbled and banked along one of the country's main highways. In reality it was no more than a country road. The speed, the music and the high walls of green bound my ears and eyes together. I was both machine and player in a real life video game and, if I was lucky, I would win. The prize? Survival.

Every so often the trees which held us in our corridor of speed dropped away and humanity scratched its imprint on nature. For a few hundred metres, single-storey wooden huts lined either side of the road. A simple shop sold a few pieces of fruit and veg and bottles of what I assume was cooking oil, the jars old and blackened by years of reuse. Here was a washed-out blue, yellow and green flag of Gabon fluttering on a makeshift flagpole. There, a hand-painted sign in garish colours announcing the village bar. There was a school with neat classrooms visible through the windowless windows. The buildings were set in an arc around a central football pitch. You would not have wanted to slide tackle on this one. Almost all these settlements had a church, another building of wood but bigger than the houses and the shops, and with the doors always open.

At random places on the road, perhaps outside someone's house, a small animal was hung upside down on a pole. 'What's the Welsh word for a hare?' Chester asked. 'Sgwarnog,' I said, 'but that's too big to be a hare.' It looked like a very small deer. Over there were a pair of black and white birds dangling from a makeshift gallows. Was the farmer-hunter advertising his morning's catch? Or was this his own evening meal simply being hung and bled? We didn't stop to find out.

At Mitzic we picked up three generations of the same family – grandmother, mother and two little girls. The children, aged about six and seven, were immaculately behaved and seemed almost scared into silence. I cannot imagine a child at home not having whined in the cramped conditions and the heat. I looked at the younger girl's jumper. It was one of those junior school designs we have back home, a polo shirt with a crest and the school's name embossed on the left-hand side. This little girl had a faded green top. I took a closer look. There was a sketch of a parent holding the hands of two children either side of him and encircling it were the words 'Ysgol Gynradd Gorseinon. Gorseinon Primary School.' When I returned home I tried to find which charity had sent a jumper from Wales to rural Gabon but my searches led me nowhere.

In addition to the family in Mitzic we also picked up several bags of grain and a five-foot-tall crop of bananas. I say 'crop' because I don't know how else to describe them. It was as if half the plant had been cut down with the broad leaves and clumps of green bananas left intact. The whole branch was piled into the back of the bus. I was sitting in the very last row, two people either side of me, a fold-down seat in front of me. I wriggled every so often to try to move the bananas out of the small of my back. It was a game of attrition between me and the yellow green beast. But whichever way I manoeuvred, some sticky sap always kissed the back of my neck as if reminding me that there was only going to be one winner in this man versus fruit competition.

When the driver changed the CD a screech like a bird's broke the short silence from the front of the bus. There was another squawk but the music dragged me back down into my slumber. I thought it was the driver's telephone ringtone or the sound of a child's handheld game. But it wasn't. When we stopped I clambered out over the usual detritus of a long bus journey, water bottles, rucksacks and half-chewed lumps of fruit. My foot nudged a plastic bag and then I saw it: a chicken, a live chicken in a plastic bag the top of which was tied around its neck.

We broke the journey again for lunch at a bend in the river called Ndjole. 'Quinze minutes,' shouted the driver. Chester and I walked across the road and up to the market. The trestle tables were overflowing with plump tomatoes, yams and mini courgettes. On another stall stood pyramids of earthy powder spice. It was inviting me to wash my hands in it. There were bananas, tomatoes, okra, pink onions, yellow and red Scotch bonnet chillies. Perched on the front of some counters were small white stones, like lumps of chalk. They can be chewed for stomach upsets. 'Especially good for women,' I was told more than once by the lady stallholders and they gave me a knowing wink. I was dazzled by the women's full-length dresses of purple, white and green. Some wore floral designs, others loud coloured prints in intricate tessellations or crazy, random geometric patterns. Some bore symbols like hieroglyphics. They wore their hair braided, the younger women with orange extensions poking out from headscarves. Others wore hats. In this weather.

On the opposite side of the road where the bank of the river flattened out they were selling fish, each about a foot long, which had been blackened on an open grill. I presumed that you took them home to reheat for supper. Maybe you could have eaten them as they were. Alongside them were knots of smaller fish stuck together through burning. Were these to be crushed into a paste to be made into a base or a stew? That night in Oyem I plucked up the courage to point at one of the black fish smoking away on a pavement grill. It was served with a good dollop of rice, which thankfully meant that vegetarian Chester also got to eat. My fish tasted pungent, as if it had almost gone off, a little like the Bombay duck you used to have in the Indian restaurants back home. If I am honest, it was just too fishy.

That afternoon at Ndjole I knelt down to get a photograph of the woman with the biggest fish. I framed it so that her ample form was framed in the curve of the river behind her left shoulder. Well, if I did. The fish wife came straight at me, knife in hand, shouting and gesticulating first at me and then at her stall. 'Please, I only wanted to take a picture of your fish,' I said hopelessly, backing off. The last thing I wanted was a public dust-up.

We walked back towards the bus, feeling like the dog scavenging on the open-air tip opposite the fish wife, tail between my legs. Chester just said, 'Poverty porn?' I knew exactly what he meant. He knew that I knew. Had we come here to a rather nothingy African country, sweated on a not-so-magic bus, simply to find the poor? To look at them with our sympathetic yet 'know nothing' eyes – and photograph them?

* * *

It was hardly going to be the match of the day. Tunisia versus Zimbabwe. Unless of course you follow football in Tunisia or Zimbabwe. And that really is what the Africa Cup of Nations, indeed all football, from Sunday league to an international jamboree like this, is all about. However second-rate your players may be and however poor your national game is, it is still your team and you support them.

We had made it back to the capital city. Tickets for the match had been advertised on giant billboards across Libreville. There were five different locations where you could buy them, apparently, though no one we spoke to seemed to think we had much of a chance of getting in. With our pidgin French we persevered, haranguing complete strangers while gesticulating at the photograph of one of the billboards that I had taken on my mobile phone. Finally, we found the one place that might be selling tickets, the Hotel de Ville on Boulevard Triumphale. We walked through the gates past an abandoned guardhouse and across the parched lawns. The main entrance though was sealed off with red and white tape as if it were a crime scene.

Feeling like intruders, we ventured around the back of the Hotel. Again we were met with blank stares by everyone until one man in a rather tight, shiny suit and wearing thin, circular spectacles took pity on us. He looked like someone out of a Guy de Maupassant short story. 'Venez ici!' he commanded, telling us to come here. And we followed the latter-day dandy down a poorly lit corridor to an annex behind the town hall itself. Room 11 was unlocked but empty. B6 was also unlocked but there was no one there either. 'Ah,' said our saviour, 'they finished at three o'clock.'

We said that he must know of someone who could offer these fans from afar a chance to watch the game. Our bespectacled friend shepherded us into the back of the main building, up a set of stairs and gestured for us to sit in a corner office. After a lengthy wait another well-dressed man was presented to us. He brandished two of the precious tickets. He told us that the price was 10,000 Central African Francs, the same price we had refused to pay the street urchins outside the shopping mall that morning. I counted out the notes and hands were shaken in thanks. Then right in front of us, without a hint of embarrassment, our middle man asked his contact for his cut of the 10,000 francs. As we walked back across the gardens, Chester again said what we were both thinking. Another game, another ticket scam and we had just helped a bent civil servant make a few quid.

We walked down the Boulevard Triumphale in silence. I looked up. Another poster was advertising the AFCON games. Instead of the list of ticket offices I had photographed earlier, this one showed the prices for each match. Oh dear.

We had just paid 5,000 francs each for tickets which were actually priced at only 500. We just laughed.

It would be easy to say that AFCON mirrors the problems of a whole continent. Africa – shambolic, sometimes corrupt and all a bit messy really. That's one interpretation of the tournament but it plays to an uncomfortable stereotype of 'all things African'. I have no doubt there are real issues in Gabon and that football administration in Africa, as elsewhere in the world, is far from perfect. One journalist described AFCON as 'beautiful, beautiful chaos'. I agree and I think even cynical Christian, in the ramshackle bar on the road from the Stade D'Amitie that first night in Gabon, could forget the politics of it all for a couple of weeks and enjoy the colour, welcome and friendship of a simple football tournament.

7

90 Minutes of Freedom

I FOLLOWED a winding footpath through the pine woods, the sun piercing the cover every so often in a flash of whiteness. Three days of wind and rain had finally abated and the forest floor was covered with autumnal leaves – some crunching, even more slushing underfoot. It smelled of damp and decay but because the sun had finally showed up I found nature's body odour uplifting rather than depressing. The path rose, droplets of water gleaming on the stumpy hazel, holly and ferns on either side. The trees parted and I was blinded by the midday sun as we walked out on to a rich grass field. This was not my usual Sunday stroll. Not a nature reserve or forestry trail. No, I was in prison. An open prison maybe but still a prison with rules, regulations, locks and uniformed officers.

HMP Prescoed near Usk is home to 230 Category D prisoners. The men are transferred here towards the end of their sentences and through education and the fostering of trust they are reintegrated into society before their release. I was here to watch one small but important element of that programme – the only prisoner football team in Wales, who today were taking on Cardiff Hibernian.

It had all been very relaxed. I made myself known at reception, had my ID copied and was asked to confirm that I had no phone on me. At the end of the tarmac drive I loitered outside the 'home' changing room and listened in as the players prepared. The imposing Ian Moore, the physical education officer and team manager, oozed authority. 'A lot of work goes into getting these teams up here to play us,' he said. 'We're a group of effing no-marks but they're not going to do a number on us.' John, the team captain and a prisoner, then had his say, 'Lads, this is our World Cup Final. I want 100 per cent effort from every one of you.' And with that, in well-worn red shirts with two diagonal white stripes, the team made their way up through the woods to the pitch on the hill.

The ground at Prescoed is in an idyllic setting, enclosed by a curtain of orange and red bushes. Raise your eyes and you see the rolling Monmouthshire hills, topped with clumps of dark green trees and the odd farmhouse. To call it a ground may be a bit of an exaggeration. There's no perimeter fence, no stand or terrace. Not that it mattered because apart from Ian, a couple of prison officers and the substitutes, the only spectators today were Jamie Grundy and me. Jamie spent a whole season following HMP Prescoed FC. His book *90 Minutes of Freedom* gives a detailed account of the men, their football and the challenges they face on and off the pitch, some of which I have recounted here. Having read their stories I had to see for myself one of these games played behind closed doors.

As they took to the field I noticed the prisoners' footwear. They wore the regulation black Hummel boots they had picked up from the rack in the changing room. One or two, however, had earned enough in prison to buy, or maybe had been gifted, smarter Adidas or Puma offerings. The touchline chatter between the players was much the same as at any local football ground. 'See that guy up front? He plays for a Welsh Prem club but he's banned at the moment. He's trying to keep up his fitness.' 'Yeah, they've got a couple of ringers in there lads. It's going to be tough today.'

The standard of play was remarkably high. Prescoed FC held their own against a team which normally played in the South Wales Alliance. But then this was a friendly. Despite the slippery pitch there was plenty of passing and some fine individual performances. One short, slightly overweight and balding midfielder for Prescoed caught my eye. He was holding up the ball and despite not running that much was delivering very good crosses. 'He played professionally in the East Midlands,' said Ian. 'Championship level. Forty-two he is and they call him Uncle Fester.' 'How long has he got left to serve?' I asked. 'He's out in January,' said Ian. 'What a pity!' And we both laughed.

Despite the normality at pitchside, the joking and cajoling, this is still a prison. Ian paced the touchline in his blue tracksuit and boots but the tell-tale sign of a long chain from his waistband to his pocket, presumably holding keys, was always there. Every so often the air would crackle as his two-way radio asked about the whereabouts of some prisoner or other. And when two of the substitutes started fooling around and a practice ball spilled on to the pitch there was a sharp 'Cut it out!' from the officer. The offenders moved on immediately. 'They're like children sometimes,' smiled Ian, indulgently.

This is Sam's first time in prison. He was sentenced for burglary with intent in an incident involving his son. He pleaded guilty the day before the trial so that the charges against his son would be dropped. 'First offence. And they put me in jail.' When he came to Prescoed, Sam started off filling the water bottles for the team and carried the first aid bag before deciding to play himself. 'I forgot where I was for a minute. It reminded me of life before prison,' he said. At 47 years of age Sam is seen as something of a father figure to the younger players who come to him and ask for help with their literacy skills. He is in no doubt as to the positive impact the team has on an offender. 'When Saturday comes it's another week off his sentence … you've got the chance to relieve a lot of tension through the football even if it's just booting the ball up in the air in training. When we win the game, we have a laugh and a joke afterwards. That's real positivity.'

By pure chance I had watched *The Loneliness of the Long Distance Runner* on a digital channel the week before I visited Prescoed. In that 1962 film a rebellious youth played by Tom Courtenay gains privileges at the borstal for his prowess at long-distance running. The governor nurtures the lad's talent with a view to have him beat a runner from a nearby public school, all for the governor's own aggrandisement. The Courtenay character plays ball and is rewarded by being allowed out of the borstal's gates to run cross-country on his own. Freedom, at least for a while.

When the big day finally comes, Courtenay is well in the lead but on the final stretch, in front of the governor and the other dignitaries, he pulls up, deliberately losing the race. As he bends over panting he stares directly at the governor.

It's a clear but self-destructive message of pride – 'You will not own me.' Needless to say the young man is sent back to the workshops and his privileged status removed. He becomes just another worthless inmate in the system. The film is a powerful depiction of class, snobbery and the abuse of power in early-1960s Britain. The tag line on the poster for the film read, 'You can play it by rules ... or you can play it by ear – what counts is that you play it right for you.' How different things are today where the inmate players and prison officers genuinely work together to rehabilitate individuals, in their own interest of course, but ultimately for the benefit of society as a whole.

Dai West is as local as I guess you can be to Prescoed. He played youth football a few miles away in Abergavenny, spent years in the military and prison service and was one of the early proponents of prison football. On the touchline the Sunday I visited he explained how the game is as much about improving the prisoners' health and well-being, their mental health particularly, as it is about winning. 'You can't sit people like this down in a classroom,' Dai said. 'Yes, it's about discipline, but football gives them all a focal point for the remainder of their sentence. There are little things like getting them to write up reports of the match or draw up league tables. It's a very basic introduction to maths or literacy. The team thing's really important too. You know we have some guys who come back from home leave to play. We have family days when the prisoners' children can come and watch dad play. It normalises things as best we can.'

Bailey is a defender for Prescoed FC. When he was transferred here from a closed prison he had been used to playing five-a-side on artificial surfaces. He says seeing the full-sized grass pitch beyond the trees was like Christmas. 'The reason I think football works here is that you can't see the prison from the pitch. For that 90 minutes or three hours you're down there, you're not in prison, and that's genuine.'

Chris, a former prisoner at Prescoed, used to play for and now coaches at Eastleigh FC in the National League. He says helping people on the inside and mentoring young players on the outside are very similar. 'Football in prison, I think it's a great release,' he said. 'I know a lot of lads, when I was in closed prison conditions, who, when they couldn't go to the gym, they'd get very anxious, they'd want to let off some steam, because some lads have long sentences or problems at home.'

The opposition are sometimes wary of playing at Prescoed. Another prisoner, Neil, says there's no reason to be afraid as the inmates have much more to lose than their rivals. 'Nobody wants to get sent back to a closed prison and there's a lot you've got to think about. Some of the teams when they come up to play us … they don't know what they're in for. But they can get away with a lot of stuff with us that we can't. If we get into an argument then anything could happen, because we're losing a lot more than just a red card. They can be a little bit dirty with us, the other teams. You've just got to bite your tongue and get on with it.'

The hopes of the men who play here are like those of all prisoners coming to the end of their sentence. They want a future when they get out, to see their children, to get a job, to not go back to jail. 'All your freedom is taken away, but football, they can't really take that away from you,' explains Tom, who is coming to the end of a seven-year sentence. Football has helped Tom and his team-mates learn to control their behaviour and develop anger-management skills. It's not easy. If they want to play for the team, the prisoners have to observe three sets of rules: those of the prison, the instructions of the PE staff and, of course, the laws of the game.

For years Prescoed FC played in the Gwent Central League and in the 2018/19 season they again won the Division Two title by 11 points. But, and this is the thing, they are only allowed to play within the prison grounds. Every game for them is a home fixture and because of this and the fact that the prisoners cannot be formally registered as players through the Football Association of Wales, even when they win the league, they cannot be promoted. When I visited Prescoed they had been kicked out of the league. There were said to be issues over the 'safeguarding' of visiting players but no one really seemed to know why. My Sunday game against Cardiff Hibs, like all their fixtures that season, was a friendly.

The pitch itself at Prescoed has an interesting history. In the run-up to the 2000 European Championships the Wales national team manager, Bobby Gould, regularly brought the squad here for training sessions. The players were staying in a nearby hotel and the Wales team's travel agent at the time had been a former 'guest' at Prescoed. On one occasion prisoners were drafted in to make the training more real, standing in a wall for free kicks and dragging defenders around the pitch. Some of Wales's favourite players, such as Gary Speed, John Hartson, Mark Hughes and Neville Southall, all trod this turf. The cost to the Football Association? A signed shirt or ball for the prison. But there's unlikely to be a return fixture. Football has moved on since the days of Mr Gould and the 'guess that will do' training facilities. The Wales manager Ryan Giggs, who also played in that team, was not so enamoured of the facilities at Prescoed. 'Prisons, school pitches, you name it. I don't want that for my players,' he has been quoted as saying. 'One of my frustrations during my Wales playing days was training on parks and bogs.'

But does prison football actually work? There's plenty of anecdotal evidence that players like it. The prison service encourages it and it is generally considered to be a good thing. That was certainly my impression on my visit to Monmouthshire. Health and well-being, education and respect were mentioned time and again. Academic studies have found a link between playing football and improved mental health. Being part of a team and sharing a common goal reduces anxiety and increases socialisation. Then there are the less tangible benefits like self-discipline, teamwork and understanding and respecting societal parameters.

Incidents of violence and assaults are lower at Prescoed than at most prisons. There were just three recorded there in the year leading up to March 2019. This may be because it is an open prison and the inmates here are, football or no football, well on their way to rehabilitation. The game is being used across the UK to counter a number of problematic issues in society – homelessness, knife crime, alcohol and substance abuse to name but a few. Even if it is just one contributory factor, it seems that the game and teams like Prescoed FC play an important part in the rehabilitation of offenders and in reducing reoffending.

Other countries certainly believe this to be the case. Dordecht prison in western Holland regularly holds tournaments for teams of serving and former prisoners. Staff and social workers also play and a few former professionals are brought in to add a touch of glamour to the event. The organiser, Gerko Brink, says, 'We try to get inmates into a new social environment with football clubs – starting out as a volunteer and if they do a good job they can be given a paid job within the club's network. It's a gift for good behaviour. So the tournament also has a motivational element.'

Prescoed FC is also proud of its links to professional football clubs. The week I visited, the players were buzzing after having had a three-day training camp with the nearest professional team, Newport County. The team's captain, John, was doing one day a week with the League Two side and is hoping to become a full-time coach when he is released.

But what of the game itself? Prescoed FC versus Cardiff Hibs. The visitors played with more confidence and their passing was more precise than the prison side. Yes the banned Welsh Premiership player scored two goals but the prison visitors had to work for their win. Prescoed missed a penalty and scored a consolation goal towards the end of the match but it ended 3-1 to Hibs. The defeat hurt as much as any other loss to any other team that weekend, perhaps more so for these players. But for many of them being a part of this team is the first time in their lives they have had to think about working with others. Football gives them a glimpse of their life before jail, a reminder of the normality that is the outside. As they trudged back to the converted stable which serves as their changing room these men were of course returning to prison, to be locked away for another night where they would dream of family and friends. But for those 90 precious minutes each one of them had escaped – even if just for a short time.

* * *

Postscript: After a public campaign by Jamie Grundy and the prison authorities the Gwent Central League allowed Prescoed FC back into Division Two for the 2020/21 season. They would have to forfeit all their away games and appoint a liaison officer to address any concerns. Whatever. The boys were back.

8

Playing Make Believe – The Wales Supporters' Team

THE SUN was still fairly high over Helsinki's Olympic Stadium when we arrived, a jumble of mildly hungover but just about willing players, joking and shuffling our way to the dressing room. I narrowed my eyes as I looked up at the stadium tower. It's an impressive structure, an example of 'formalist' architecture from the 1930s'. The tower is 72.71m high, the length of the gold medal-winning javelin throw by Finland's Matti Järvinen in the 1932 Olympics. This afternoon's sporting feat was also to be a landmark, if just a little less impressive. For this was 7 September 2002 and the very first match of the Wales Supporters' Team.

The idea of a fans' team was conceived by a few regular Wales followers over a beer in a bar in Yerevan the previous year. After that game in Armenia, Wales's next competitive match would be the first of the Euro 2004 qualifying campaign, away to Finland. A message was posted on a Finnish supporters' message board and the die was cast. Game on. We had a truly representative squad for that first match as 20 players from all over Wales stepped up to the challenge. There was a half-decent trio from Aberystwyth – Gareth Bailey, the 16-year-old keeper from Llandudno, Stu from Wrexham, Bryn from Anglesey – and a few of us veterans from Cardiff. Chester was seven years old and became our team mascot. 'Stick him on the wing,' shouted Ade Colley at half-time when the Wales team was already a couple of goals down. A few dozen stray Wales supporters had also ventured to the edge of the city to cheer us on. They laughed, waved flags and guzzled beer on the touchline. I guess that afternoon set the tone for all our supporters' matches to come.

We had no excuses on that sunny autumn afternoon. There were properly qualified referees and the pitch was immaculate. 'The best I've ever played on,' said my friend Gron, who was by then an ageing member of Poynton Rangers FC. Mark Hughes's team had warmed up on this very ground just hours earlier. Its magic worked for him and the real Wales team went on to win 2-0 that evening. But our rag-bag squad of pot-bellied fans were no match for the sprightly young Finns and we lost 7-2. Maybe we should have picked Chester after all. At the final whistle our hosts graciously invited us into the sauna with them. Inexperienced as we then were in international sporting diplomacy, we politely declined. Ninety minutes of football had been hot enough for us. Despite the scoreline a good time was had by all and the Wales Supporters' Team was born.

Since that glorious inglorious day in Helsinki the fans' team has played more than 100 times on foreign turf and in some cases rocky sand. Our next away game was a year later before Wales played Serbia and Montenegro as the country was then called. It was a slightly nervy visit. The country was still finding its feet after the Balkan wars. Britain and the US had fairly recently bombed Belgrade in the dispute over Kosovo. This Euro qualifier had been postponed after Serbia's prime minister, Zoran Đinđić, was killed by a single sniper's shot as he walked into the main government building. Many of the Wales supporters had already booked flights so they travelled to Belgrade anyway. There they played the locals and got a creditable 1-1 draw.

Four months later we were back in Serbia for the match 'proper'. The supporters played on the same rough pitch in Novi Beograd. Keen to be seen to be extending the hand of friendship and building bridges with the Serbs, the British ambassador himself had turned up with his children to play. They emerged from a bulletproof car and had a minder close at hand. The younger son made a bit of a faux pas by wearing his England football socks. Her Majesty's representatives may have impressed the locals by being there but wearing any sort of England kit at any sort of Wales game didn't help them ingratiate themselves with the Welsh fans.

That second match against Serbia was notable for another reason. The game was not going to plan and we were a few goals down very early on. From my right-back position I looked over for guidance to our manager, Neil Dymock. Nothing. He was busy texting on the sideline. Unbeknown to us, Neil had met the former Wales internationals Dave Philips and Malcolm Allen the previous night. 'Come and play for the supporters tomorrow,' he said, half-seriously. 'We'll only turn up if you are truly desperate,' was their reply. We were and they did, arriving in a taxi just before the second half got under way. Chester, who was now eight years old, got on to play for the last few minutes when the game was well and truly lost. He is convinced he put a pass through to Allen who went on to score. It made little difference as the plucky Welsh went down 9-6. What Neil hadn't told us was that the opposition 'fans' team was actually a proper Serbian third division outfit.

These supporters' games soon became a fixture of the Wales Away trips. Sometimes we were down to the bare bones of a team and then we would have two dozen players on the touchline, each one vying for 20 minutes of glory in a red shirt. We played in Russia, Latvia, Azerbaijan, Austria, the Basque Country, the USA and Bulgaria, indeed anywhere our national team played and where the locals could field a team. Every so often Neil would magic up a former international to play for 20 minutes or even a full half. In Merthyr our national team manager Chris Coleman made an appearance in a fundraising game against the Football Association of Wales staff team. He may not have been as mobile as he once was but somehow he knew just where to position himself and he headed the ball further than I could kick it.

As if to confirm ourselves as a permanent, if not necessarily top, international team, the supporters invited themselves to the 2008 Eurofan tournament. This celebration of football and friendship is the brainchild of Oleg Soldatenko, who supports the Ukrainian club Karpaty Lviv. Lvov, or Lviv as it is called in Ukrainian, is the self-styled cultural capital of western Ukraine. With its cobbled streets, fine universities and graceful yellow Habsburg buildings you feel you are on a film set, rather like Prague before the tourists arrived. Lviv was left unscathed despite being occupied by both the

Soviets and the Germans during the Second World War and is now a UNESCO World Heritage site.

Eurofan attracts teams from across Europe and for Oleg and his friends it is an opportunity to shake off some of the grim images we may have of the game out east in a country desperate to display its European credentials. For us supporters, it is a chance to play and socialise with other fans in a beautiful and slightly exotic city. The results, on or off the pitch, frankly, take a back seat. British teams have done pretty well in Lviv. Glasgow Rangers supporters won the tournament in 2009. Liverpool too have played here and the Wales team once reached the quarter-finals. Okay, we didn't win the group to get there but went through after the Polish team was arrested en masse following the stabbing of a doorman in the Millennium nightclub. The official Eurofan website notes that the Poles withdrew due to 'technical reasons'.

The Wales team visited Lviv six times and initiated charity visits by the teams attending Eurofan. Supporters from each country would raise money and visit children's homes with gifts of sports kit, toiletries and sweets. John O'Neill, the captain of the Republic of Ireland team, told me how his players had raised more than €600. 'The lads really got into it. This is our chance to give something back to this city. The craic is great here and everyone is so welcoming,' he said.

Some of the friendships we made at Eurofan lasted way beyond the final whistle. Wales had a knack of drawing the Republic in the qualifying groups and we have played John and his team at their Irishtown 'base' in Dublin as well as offering them a welcome when they come to Cardiff. We got on so well with Machiel and his team from SC Heerenveen in Friesland that a year later we travelled to Holland to play in their annual five-a-side tournament. That night our Dutch friends provided tickets for us to watch their team in action in the Eredivisie. They then brought a team over to Wales for a friendly match in Cardiff.

Football away-days are shambolic, drink-fuelled, boisterous, non-stop parties. That's why we love them. But the supporters' games offer a chance to see a different side of the country we visit, away from the city centre cafes and bars. They have also given me some of my most memorable experiences on a pitch. In Belgium I had the privilege of playing alongside Gary Lloyd. In Welsh footballing circles Gary is something of a legend. He played more than 500 times in our top flight for Barry Town, Carmarthen and his hometown club Llanelli. Gary was the first Welsh Premier League footballer to be called into the full Wales squad and was inducted into the Welsh Premier League Hall of Fame in 2012. He can now add to his CV scoring a goal for the supporters' team.

On that pitch in Brussels before yet another vital qualifying match for the senior squad, Gary faced one of his most serious sporting challenges – shepherding me through 90 minutes of football. He patiently talked me, an absolute amateur, through the game. 'Step up with me, Tim,' he said. 'Let the winger go. That's it. He's got to come to you. Good. Stick with me.' What a teacher, what a gentleman. Some years later Gary suffered a stroke. A testimonial match was played for him at Barry Town and it was great to see so many friends and players, many from the fans' team, turn up at Jenner Park to support him.

It may be the price of the beer but some of the best times we have had as a team have been 'out east'. A pre-Euro warm-up in Kiev in 2016 offered us a chance to renew our friendship with the Ukrainians. The hospitality started before we had even got changed. In the middle of the dressing room a table had been laid out with trays of food and snacks, sliced meats and pickles, crackers, chocolate. On the floor were slabs of beer and bottles of local brandy. Was this a ploy? Post-match beers we had come to expect, but drinks before kick-off? Naughty. Thankfully, we made it on to the pitch without giving in to temptation. And what a good decision that was.

We were 3-0 down at half-time but the Wales team is nothing if not resilient and we played through the previous night's beer to draw 3-3. Fair result and honour served, you might think. Oh no. Our hosts had different ideas. They wanted a result and said we must take it to penalties but strangely they said only three kicks. Perhaps they had three great strikers and wanted to win it quickly. In the event Tom Bowen kept his cool, picked his side and beat the keeper. Wales won 3-2 on penalties. We ran on to the pitch diving on top of each other and burying little Tom in a sweaty pile as if we had won the actual Euros.

As we walked back to the dressing room and our Ukrainian feast that afternoon in Kiev, our captain, Dave O'Gorman, came over to me and pointed at a middle-aged man in a rather tight yellow and blue kit, one of their players. I liked the fact that he was about my age, okay maybe a little younger than me, but we were both still willing to give it a go. 'Do you know who that is, Tim?' said Dave, reverentially. 'Recognise him?' I did not. 'He's Oleg Salenko. He won the

Golden Boot at the 1994 World Cup.' I was stunned. Here was a true footballing legend. Salenko scored five goals in one game, Russia's 6–1 win against Cameroon. He scored one more goal in the tournament and shared the Golden Boot with Hristo Stoichkov. Salenko also played for three different countries – the USSR, Ukraine and Russia. Now he had played against Wales. And I had played against him.

What is it then about playing for the fans' team that makes me and everyone who gets a chance to do so, so very proud? The standard of the football is variable to say the least. The arrangements can be shambolic, sometimes frustrating. But it is our team and this is our chance to pull on the red shirt, to sing the anthem like our heroes and to give our all for Wales. Make believe? Maybe, but I just love it.

9

You Are Not Welcome Here

MY IRISH brother-in-law, Pat, says I have a romanticised view of football, that I can only see the good, the communal and the uplifting side of the game. He points to tribalism and the divisions which a club or a national team can embody and inflame. 'Don't get me wrong. I love the game but it can be a force for bad too,' he says. I guess he's thinking about the religious overtones of a Rangers v Celtic derby, the racist banners of Beitar Jerusalem FC and the images of marauding hooligans we see at a European fixture every few years.

We all crave the atmosphere that two sets of supporters create, fomenting a cauldron of partisanship and passion. But there's a fine line between football 'banter' and real intimidation. When Cardiff City play Nottingham Forest I join the chant of 'scabs, scabs' at the opposition. It's a reference to the 1984 miners' strike when the Nottinghamshire colliers went back to work while the south Wales pits held firm. Is that harmless fun or incitement? Here is a more recent and more serious example of how the game can be hijacked for political ends. In late 2020 the press officer for the Azerbaijan champions, Qarabağ FK, posted online, 'We must kill all Armenians. Children, women, the elderly, showing no regret nor compassion. If we do not kill them, they will kill us and our children.' How can this have anything to do with football?

Pat is right that football can be hijacked for nationalistic, political or religious ends, but not about my turning a blind eye to it. Much as I might want to, I cannot avoid it. Neither can the game itself. UEFA has a list of 'forbidden' matches, which cannot be played because of the mayhem that might ensue. Ukraine cannot draw Russia, no Armenia v Azerbaijan or Spain against Gibraltar. In Scotland, Supporters Direct campaigns against those who use religious divisions to turn football into a vehicle for hatred. Following my club, Cardiff, I have had to endure 'bubble' matches. When the police believe the threat of trouble between opposing fans is too high, every one of us is forced to travel in a single, escorted convoy to the ground. Once at the stadium we are sealed into the stand and then escorted firmly home.

The annual Eurofan tournament in Lviv badges itself as the friendly football festival. Fans' teams from across Europe play and then socialise together but even at this level there are hints of the dark side of football. During the 2009 tournament, when I played there with the Wales Supporters' Team, I saw three black players blocked from returning to an enclosed training pitch to collect their shin pads. 'You are not welcome here,' said a Polish skinhead in broken English, as he made a gesture as if slitting his throat.

In the following year's tournament, the Wales team lost their group match 9-1 in a bruising encounter against the

Ukrainian fans, but all was forgotten as the players left the field. The Ukrainian midfielder struggled to pull off his drenched jersey. He had the words 'White Hooligan' tattooed across his belly in old Germanic script (it's interesting that across Europe these fans' slogans, chants, and now tattoos, are in English – an embarrassing salute to the birthplace of football hooliganism, often referred to as the 'English disease'). On the back of his neck the Ukrainian had inked a blue cross and a circle, the symbol of white power. He was big and he looked mean, but was remarkably friendly. We discussed all things football and the price of the local beer, though I did not seek out his company in the bar that night.

There were some interesting juxtapositions at Eurofan. At the same caged pitch where I had witnessed racism, the red hand of Ulster flew alongside the Irish Republic's tricolour behind the goal. I couldn't see that happening too easily in Belfast or Dublin. That afternoon was a colourful celebration of everyone's shared passion for football. Most of us left our politics and religion in the dressing room. All of us were there to win but when a team's numbers were depleted through injury or too much Lvivskyi beer, players from different nations stepped into the breach to make sure there was a full side. 'Our team should be renamed the United Nations,' said the Wales coach, Neil Dymock. 'We had two Georgians, a Dane and a couple of Ukrainians play for us.'

That year's final pitted the Bulgaria supporters against fans of Romania's Dinamo Bucharest. One man's shirt caught my eye as he stomped up and down the touchline. He was in his late 40s and about 16 stone but had just about squeezed into his football jersey. He was the Bulgaria team manager. Printed in Cyrillic script on the back of his shirt was the word 'ДУЧЕ' (Duce), a nod to Italian fascist leader Benito Mussolini. Below that were printed the numbers 8 8. The eighth letter of the alphabet is H, and H H is code among fascists for 'Heil Hitler'. After a week of great football and friendship, it left a bitter taste.

Sadly, the problem of racism in football only really makes the headlines when it hits the big stage of the professional game, television audiences and all that. Around the same time that we were playing in Lviv, Holland played Poland in a warm-up match before the European finals. The Dutch captain, Mark van Bommel, said that during the game his black players had been subjected to monkey chants from the crowd. The Dutch FA said the chanting was mixed with Polish fans making political statements. Deeply offensive yes, but they would be making no official complaint 'for the good of the game'. Really?

It may be unfair to single out one country. England have been fined for booing during the opposing team's national anthem. In 2017, when the Three Lions played Germany in Dortmund, fans went on the rampage. The papers described the city as 'a war zone'. Italy too has problems. Inter Milan's Romelu Lukaku was subjected to the ugliest kind of racist taunts during his first season in Serie A. Quoted in *GQ* after one particularly ugly match against Cagliari, Lukaku, the son of Congolese immigrants to Belgium, said that the football authorities have allowed a culture of racism to fester. 'Ladies and gentlemen it's 2019, instead of going forward, we're going backwards,' he said.

But Bulgaria does seem to have, if not a persistent, then definitely a more visible, problem with racism than many other European countries. In 2011 the Bulgarian Football Union (BFU) was fined after England players Ashley Young, Ashley Cole and Theo Walcott were subjected to racist abuse. In 2013, halfway through a domestic match, fans of Levski Sofia unveiled a banner wishing Adolf Hitler a happy birthday. On my last visit to the Bulgarian capital for Wales's Nations Cup game there, the neighbourhood we stayed in was plastered with the graffiti of SW99, a hooligan faction belonging to Levski.

When England played them in a Euro 2020 qualifying game their black players were again subjected to racist chants and Nazi salutes. The Bulgarians were already halfway through a two-game ban after being found guilty of racist behaviour in matches against the Czech Republic. That England game had to be stopped on two occasions. The BFU was fined and ordered to play two matches behind closed doors (with one of those suspended for two years). Despite some embarrassing prevarication the president of the BFU, Borislav Mihaylov, resigned, but only after being told to quit by the prime minister, Boyko Borissov.

The troublemakers are of course a minority and most supporters condemn them, but there is a strange logic surrounding football and racism. Hardcore Bulgarian fans say they would not racially abuse local opposition teams while they too had black players on their own side. A famous Levski supporter was quoted saying that he does not like African-Americans, Turkish people and Arabs, but he does not mind the dark-skinned football players of Levski. It is as if their hatred is reserved mainly for international fixtures, that they are making some sort of national declaration.

Kamen Alipiev, a reporter based in Sofia, told the BBC that it is easy to see hooliganism and racism as isolated phenomena with football merely providing a convenient outlet. But he says there are wider societal issues at work. Alipiev says that in Bulgaria these problems, such as unemployment, migration and housing, get easily conflated, 'We have problems with communications with our Roma Gypsies in the area, with refugees coming from Asia and Africa … so maybe sometimes it sounds like it's normal.' Okay, but how many times have we in Britain heard the same line, 'I'm not racist but …?' It just won't wash any longer.

The Bulgarian Centre for the Study of Democracy (CSD) produced a report called 'Radicalisation in Bulgaria: Threats and Trends' which looked at the issue of racism and football. Researchers found links between supporters and far-right nationalist movements. Dr Atanas Rusev said that during street protests some football fans had been mobilised to attack Roma communities and that many of those involved in the racist abuse against the England team in 2013 were part of Levski Sofia's SW99 hooligan faction. The abuse at the Euro qualifier, they concluded, was planned. There is also another motive. The CSD researchers say that some supporters with a history of racist behaviour demand payment from clubs in order to stop.

After the 2013 England game there was much hand-wringing and condemnation from the football authorities. The president of UEFA, Aleksander Čeferin, said that the 'football family' and governments needed to 'wage war on the racists'. I wrote at the time that the game was not taking this issue seriously, that token fines and partial closures of grounds as punishment were too lenient. What we need is a sliding scale of real sanctions against countries and clubs to demonstrate that we will not tolerate behaviour like this. It's not that difficult. How about full ground closures, a ban on travelling fans, points deductions and ultimately exclusion from all international competition? That would be painful for supporters and associations alike. And so it should be. Recognising the problem for what it is and acting decisively would of course be a blow to the prestige of UEFA and its vaunted diversity and equality initiatives. None of this is happening though. So let's be frank. They don't really care do they?

There is a 'code of honour' among hooligans which I don't quite understand but for which I was once very grateful. In October 2015 I joined a sponsored drive by the Wales supporters' charity, Gôl Cymru, to Bosnia. The day before our European qualifying game we visited two children's homes in the city of Zenica where the game was being played. Alongside the usual football kits and toys, we bought them washing machines and other white goods. Local television crews were in attendance and though embarrassed by all the fuss, we smiled and shook hands for the cameras. Job done.

We had been warned by the police not to hang around Zenica on matchday as there was a crowd of hooligans called the Robijaši (Prisoners) associated with the NK Čelik club who were said to be intent on creating trouble. 'Stay in Sarajevo. Get the organised bus to the game,' was the advice. 'You'll be safe then.' But did we listen? Clad in our red Wales shirts, a small crowd of us arrived early the next day and sat in a sports bar avoiding the driving rain.

You couldn't miss us. I'd had a couple of beers when Mark Ainsbury, one of the London Welsh contingent, came over and said someone wanted to see me. 'They say he's their top boy, but everything's okay,' he whispered. I knew no one in Zenica. 'Top boy?' I knew that was some ridiculous hooligan expression. Why hadn't I listened to the advice?

A man in his late 20s walked across the bar. Dressed in black, he exuded a confidence just short of a swagger. He held out his hand. 'I want to thank you,' he said. 'Normally you would not make it to here from the station but we saw you boys on television last night. With the children. We are grateful. I have told all the boys "no trouble with the Welsh".

'Oh, and sorry about the flag,' he added, referring to a Welsh dragon which had been stolen from a group of fans and paraded upside down on social media by masked Bosnian ultras. With that he shook my hand again and left.

For travelling supporters the fear of violence is disproportionate to the actual risk of seeing any trouble. During the 2016 European Championship, Russian hooligans went on the rampage in Marseille, attacking English fans in what some called 'organised' attacks. There was even talk of state involvement by Russia. I was genuinely shocked by the videos I saw online. Some of the hooligans filmed themselves running through the streets of the old town hitting and kicking anyone who happened to be there. There was one dreadful image of an old man on his way home from the shops being beaten to the ground and left unconscious.

By the time we got to Toulouse for Wales's group match against Russia I was quietly scared for my safety. I was not the only one. The city's mayor had decreed that for security reasons our fans' game would have to be played outside the city limits. It was a seriously sunny day and Chester and I had to take two buses and then a long walk to get to the pitch. For once the fans' teams were evenly matched and the game ended in a 3-3 draw. I was proud that Wales's three goals were all scored by Sion Cox, a fine player I had managed for ten years as a child in the Urdd teams back in Cardiff.

At the final whistle a middle-aged Russian player came up to me and gestured at Chester who was standing near me. 'Father and son?' Someone with a little English translated for us. 'Yes, he's my boy. Great that we can still play together, isn't it?' I replied. 'Father and son!' said the man and wrapped his arm around another young player. Here we were, two fathers, two sons playing football, enjoying the Euros, no edge, no fear. We four had a couple of beers and communicated as best we could about the fans' game and our nations' prospects for the big match later that day. We were genuinely sorry we could not stay and enjoy their hospitality but Mr Mayor's decree meant we had another hour's travel to get back into town. After all the bad press the Russians had received I felt a little peevish that I had branded them all as potential hooligans, people to avoid.

10

Whose Game Is It Anyway?

THERE WAS something rather prophetic about the end of the 2014/15 season. United States federal prosecutors had announced the indictment of more than a dozen officials of the game's continental football governing bodies, CONMEBOL (South America), and CONCACAF (Caribbean, Central and North America) along with some sports marketing executives. They were accused of collusion in the allocation of rights for high-profile international competitions.

In Europe there were also allegations of criminal mismanagement and misappropriation in the game. 'Rotten to the core' screamed the papers. Sepp Blatter would ultimately lose his position as president of FIFA. The other players pleaded guilty in the US and forfeited more than $40m as part of their pleas. Evidence if ever it were needed of the way the game has not only been tainted by greed but driven by it. Could these moves be the start of the clean-up we had all been waiting for?

I think we have all turned a blind eye to excesses at the top of football. The machinations of the governing bodies are opaque, the figures involved just too big for us to process. It all seems way above our heads as we grumble about the price of a pint down the stadium or an away-day to Leeds. Like the wider economy we have tended to say, 'These decisions are not for the likes of us.' I just want to watch my team and not worry about the rest of it. But we should.

Football was an early proponent of supply side economics. The 'trickle down' theory states that reducing taxes and encouraging the wealthy to become more wealthy means some of those gains come down to the rest of us. Society and the wider game will progress if you just let those in charge have a free rein. The idea has been around since the end of the Second World War and was particularly favoured by President Reagan and Margaret Thatcher.

I don't believe this theory for one reason. Never mind the moral argument of making the rich richer, 'trickle down' simply does not work, particularly in football. Below the criminality of FIFA and UEFA, just look at the wealth in the Premier League compared with the rest of the domestic game. Local clubs are closing for the cost of one Premier League player's weekly wage. Trickle-down economics? Crumbs from the top table more like. The effective privatisation of the game through putting corporate and personal interests above those of the game itself is, not so slowly, killing it. The alarm bells were ringing in 2015 at, of all places, the Cardiff City Stadium.

I guess you would have expected the then-chairman of the Football Association, Greg Dyke, to have his two penn'orth over that FIFA scandal. 'Blatter-bashing' became a national pastime for a couple of days with cabinet ministers, sports administrators and retired footballers all having their say. But perhaps Dyke should have looked a little closer to home before having a go at football's world governing body for bowing down before corporate interests, the Swiss franc or the dollar or whichever currency FIFA's members want their bungs.

Speaking of Blatter, Dyke said, 'I'm already taking bets he won't be there in four years. When the American attorney general says this is the beginning, not the end, she is right. There is a lot more to come out.' One thing then that Greg and I were in agreement with but two small and seemingly unrelated incidents at the time made me wince when I heard him speak. Both showed the way the 'beautiful game' was not just moving away from its traditional fanbase but actually alienating them.

In May 2015, Cardiff City played Blackpool in their last home game of the season and, not surprisingly, the Blackpool fans used the occasion to vent their anger at the way the Oyston family was running the club. Dad, mum and then son Oyston had been accused of taking money out of the club while the historic Bloomfield Road ground crumbled and the players were forced to wash their own kits. Cue a noisy but peaceful protest by the away fans in the Welsh capital. Banners were unfurled reading 'Oyston Out'. The stewards acted immediately. They took down the banners and ejected several fans.

It's worth noting that the Cardiff fans joined in with the chanting and applauded the Blackpool supporters in solidarity. I took up the issue of the ejections with the management at Cardiff City. Despite there having been no complaint by any travelling fan, the club said that it would not tolerate banners that were 'political, discriminatory, offensive or inflammatory'.

How, I asked, are the words 'Oyston Out' any of the above? I was told that it was all done 'on the basis of respect for our visiting directors' position'. So, no offence was caused to the 2,000 visiting fans but *possibly* to two visiting directors. It begged the question: who is the game of football for? Directors in the hospitality box or the Blackpool faithful who have been treated with contempt by their own club and now simply want to protest about it? I was reminded of the time I took Cardiff's owner Vincent Tan to task about his decision to change the club's playing colours from blue to red and to replace the 100-year-old Bluebird crest with a dragon. 'You don't like it?' he said, 'then find yourself a new owner.'

Roll on a couple of weeks to the 2015 FA Cup Final. Two of football's historic names, Aston Villa and Arsenal, were to meet at Wembley, the home of football. The final has always been the pinnacle of the domestic football season. A few days before the big game I watched Greg Dyke being interviewed by Gary Lineker in one of those lengthy preview programmes the BBC love to produce to exploit their dwindling sports rights. 'Hasn't the game been tarnished by the way tickets for Wembley don't go to supporters but to sponsors and corporates?' ventured Lineker. 'And why play the game at 5.30 when we all know that football is traditionally played at three o'clock on a Saturday afternoon?'

Dyke was keen to do something about the ticket allocation, and yes, they were looking at getting more fans in. After all, 25,000 to each team in an 80,000-seater stadium does seem a bit mean (the other 30,000 of course go to 'the game' and, that's right, sponsors). But Dyke's answer to the question of kick-off time was quite amazing. 'Ah,' said Dyke, 'it's the television people. They say they get a bigger audience at 5.30 and, well, what are we to do?'

The answer Greg is in the name. The 'FA' Cup. Yes, that's the same Football Association of which you were chairman. Just say no, take less money if needs be, maintain the tradition of the cup and stick to a three o'clock kick-off. It was a pat answer which said a lot about football's priorities and which too few of us are willing to challenge. Dyke's complacency on television's dominant role and the bully-boy tactics at Cardiff were two small illustrations of the way the game is only interested in those who have money, those with clout and to hell with the people who make it what it is.

Roll on five years to 2020 and the Covid pandemic offered a perfect opportunity to reset the game. As the 2019/20 season shut down we could all take stock and address the underlying problems facing football. Now was the ideal time to introduce independent regulation, a fit and proper directors test, salary caps for players maybe, rein in the agents, to have supporter directors on the boards of our clubs and to promote community ownership. Good ideas whose time had come? No chance. While infections spiralled, businesses shut down and fans everywhere faced economic uncertainty, what did we get? Football without fans at last became a reality.

Clubs were desperate to finish the season and of course to fulfil those television contracts. And so they did. The televised games had no crowds but they did have canned crowd noise. Some clubs placed cardboard cutouts of supporters where we used to sit. You could actually pay to have your own image placed in your seat and you could also buy an electronic programme to read in the comfort of your home as you tried to spot yourself on the small screen. The season ended. There was promotion and relegation. It was a win-win all round, wasn't it?

When the new season finally got under way, again behind closed doors, the Premier League went one better and asked fans, many of whom had already bought season tickets for their club, for Sky Sport and for BT, to fork out £14.95 per game to watch matches not already scheduled for TV. To show how seriously out of touch the top of the game is with reality, in October they unveiled 'Project Big Picture'. Driven by Liverpool and Manchester United, this reset of the national game would have involved the Premier League being reduced from 20 to 18 clubs. Power would be vested in the nine clubs that have remained in the league longest and a group of six of them would be able to approve a TV deal or veto any new owner of a club. Never mind the FA Cup Final at 5.30pm, under this plan all Premier League clubs could sell eight live matches a season directly to fans from their own channels. Another subscription, anyone?

At last there was outrage from the football family. Describing the plan as a 'sugar-coated cyanide pill', the Football Supporters' Association said, 'The insatiable greed of a small handful of billionaire owners cannot be allowed to determine the structure of football in this country. Their desire to stitch things up behind closed doors, without even speaking to their fellow clubs, let alone fans, makes crystal clear the urgent need for the Government's promised fan-led review of football governance.' For once the FA showed up too. Its chairman, Greg Clarke, said the plan would mean 'the concentration of power and wealth in the hands of a few clubs with a breakaway league mooted as a threat'. The FA, he said, would block any such move and bar rebel clubs from European competition. In an acrimonious meeting, all 20 Premier League clubs met and decided unanimously to reject the project.

So that was that. Well, not quite. Just a week after the Big Picture was torn up, the top clubs were at it again. Those working-class bastions of solidarity, Liverpool and Manchester United, had been in further secret talks to form a breakaway European Super League. Teams from Italy, France, Germany and Spain were said to be part of the plan which would be funded to the tune of £4.6bn by the Wall Street bank J.P. Morgan. FIFA was said to have approved the plan but UEFA said any changes to its existing open-format competitions were 'non-negotiable'.

The idea for a European Super League has been around for more than 20 years and, despite the damage it would inflict on the integrity of existing European competitions, not to mention each country's domestic set-up, like some beastly Hydra it continues to raise its ugly head. I would argue that such a league is the inevitable next step for a game which is effectively bullied by those who, blinded by the billions that flow their way, cannot see the value of football below the very top tier. Theirs is a game controlled by the sale of television rights and sponsorship deals. Anything below that is just not important.

I am exhausted by this relentless 'trickle up' approach to our national game. Sad as it may be to say goodbye to the sacred 92, the indivisible football pyramid, the magic of the cup and the community game, should we the supporters now just say to the big boys, 'Off you go. We'll take our chances.'? Because only then, freed of their greed and contempt for the rest of us, will we be able to begin to reclaim the heart and soul of the game.

11

Beyond The Scaffold

SOME TEAMS pride themselves on their political affiliation as much as for their football. On the left we have FC St. Pauli in Germany which painted 'No Football for Fascists' across one of its stands. On the right, Zenit St Petersburg from Russia, whose fans sometimes wear Ku Klux Klan-style hoods to matches and which, in the run-up to the 2018 World Cup, was branded by *The Sun* as 'the world's most racist football club'. Such radical and public sentiments sit uneasily here where the mantra has for so long been that we must keep politics out of football. On the other hand there are some clubs and supporters who think the two should be inseparable and in 2014 I got to see how activism and football can make for a happy, if somewhat bizarre, marriage.

My son Chester was living in London and had thrown his lot in with Clapton FC. His contempt for professional football and the modern game led him to this allegedly more authentic sporting experience. 'This is what it's all about, Dad,' he enthused. 'Not big stars on ridiculous money, all-seater stadiums, bolshie stewards and police restrictions. Forget all that branding and replica shirt stuff. The real thing is down there in Clapton. Football's not dead. You've got to come see it for yourself.' And so I did.

Forest Gate, in the London borough of Newham, is hardly the first place you would look for a footballing revolution. Hidden behind a rather run-down tyre fitters, the only sign of the uprising was a crumbling wooden sign that read 'Clapton Football Club'. Inside the Old Spotted Dog Ground, clouds of dust blew around as the players warmed up. The nets were ancient and the linesman wore a cardigan, long trousers and trainers. He was standing in for the 'official' official who had been caught in that day's tube strike.

But as soon as the game kicked off, so did the Clapton Ultras. Red smoke bombs blotted out the pitch and a bizarre version of 'When the Saints Go Marching In' rattled off the roof of the tiny terrace: 'Oh east London, is wonderful. Oh east London, is wonderful. It's full of pies, mash and Clapton. Oh east London is wonderful.' A hundred or so supporters had squeezed under a dodgy roof of corrugated sheets held up by a pile of rusting scaffold poles. The self-proclaimed 'Scaffold Brigada' have turned Clapton games into a riot of colour, noise, tins of lager and general good times.

Eton Manor had not seen anything like this in the Essex Senior League. Neither had I. As their keeper stepped gingerly through the thick grass and nettles behind the goal to retrieve the ball, another chant swept across the ground. 'RMT, RMT, RMT' to the tune of 'Here We Go' rang out in praise of the transport workers' union which had again crippled the London Underground. This was closely followed by a full rendition of Billy Bragg's anthem 'Power in a Union'.

Dressed in a duffle coat with a rolled cigarette hanging from his lip, John Venners waved a flag with 'Anti-Fascist Alliance' hand painted in red and white on a black background. Another homemade banner read 'Sometimes anti-social. Always anti-fascist.' These wannabe revolutionaries wear their hearts on their sleeves and those hearts are firmly on the left. Rumour had it that the local English Defence League thugs would come down to 'sort out the commies', but nothing so far had happened.

In my 1970s heyday we had all manner of political causes to shout about. There was General Pinochet, gay rights and apartheid in South Africa. Maggie was heading for power and the Welsh language was dying on its feet. This generation was supporting Clapton FC – and the transport workers' union. Clapton is not alone in blending style, social activism and left-wing politics with football. The trend started on mainland Europe decades ago. Germany has a string of so-called 'Kult' clubs. St. Pauli were an early example and used the location of its ground near the famous Reeperbahn, in the socially mixed docks area of Hamburg, to its advantage. In the 1980s, a trendy, alternative fan scene grew around the club. Supporters adopted the skull and crossbones flag, the symbol the city's squatters had used, as their own. As fascist-inspired hooliganism spread across Germany, St. Pauli were the first club to officially ban any sort of right-wing displays in its Millerntor-Stadion.

In Spain, Rayo Vallecano play in a traditionally working-class area east of Madrid. Their fanbase is staunchly left wing and opposes the commercialisation of modern football.

In 2014 fans and players came together and raised funds to rehouse an 85-year-old woman who was being evicted by police because of the financial crisis. The Italian Communist Party was founded in Livorno in 1921 so it is no surprise that a century later fans of its football club wave Palestinian banners and belt out 'Bandiera Rossa' (The Red Flag).

Clapton has reached out and made links with like-minded European clubs. In April 2019, to celebrate the 80th anniversary of the end of the Spanish Civil War, they travelled to Barcelona to play Club Esportiu Júpiter from the fifth tier of Spanish football. The visitors' strip of red, yellow and purple was inspired by the flag of the Second Spanish Republic and the International Brigades whose foreign volunteers joined the anti-fascist fight against General Franco. CE Júpiter play in the working-class Poblenou suburb and during the 1930s had links to anarchist trade unions. It is said that during the civil war the ground was used to store guns and ammunition. Its enemy today is the Madrid government and its cause, Catalan independence.

Note that these clubs all play in their country's second tier or below. In the English game you have to go through the leagues to find a 'Kult' team. Alongside Clapton you have Dulwich Hamlet FC who play in the National League South, and whose fans call themselves 'The Rabble'. When the FA chairman Greg Clarke resigned after making racist and sexist remarks in front of a committee of MPs, the club's official Twitter account said, 'It's 2020, and we still have a lot of work to do in football to root out Racism, Sexism and Homophobia … Things need to change, and clearly that change needs to happen at the top.' There is also a growing number of supporter-owned clubs like Merthyr Town FC and AFC Wimbledon. FC United of Manchester were set up by disgruntled Manchester United fans fed up with the way the game and their club was being hijacked for purely commercial reasons.

I love this brand of punk football, if true punk can be a brand. Not everyone, however, is happy with this trendification of the game. Traditionalists accuse the self-styled ultras of hopping on a hipster bandwagon. There was certainly a whiff of Spitalfields chic about the grungy beards and combat trousers on parade when I went down the Old Spotted Dog. This was designer Red before the fashion labels moved in. My journalist friend Ade too was a little sceptical. 'It seems a bit post-student to me,' he said. 'Let's see how many of them are here in three years' time.' But take away the politics and it is football as pure entertainment and self-made at that. Isn't that what it's supposed to be all about?

Clapton were 2-0 down within 20 minutes but the fans didn't care. Up went a chorus reviling Maggie Thatcher and praising Tony Benn. At last, a reference from my day that I could relate to. Someone used the c-word in a chant. A bald-headed young man from the back shouted loudly but politely, 'Come on, guys, didn't we agree last week not to use that word?' 'Yeah, right. Sorry,' came a sheepish voice from behind the Scaffold. And the chant stopped dead.

The level of support under the Scaffold was pretty remarkable given that Clapton were in the ninth tier of English football and the players were not paid. The 'Tons' ended that season in the wilderness known as the middle of the table. But how to explain the fanatical support from the wobbly terrace? Are the Ultras a grassroots movement revolting against modern football and the marginalisation of the real fan? Or is it just a trendy way of raising two fingers to the world, a safe form of left-wing gesture politics?

Oddly, Clapton's owner at the time was not too pleased with the attention his team was getting. The fans had started asking questions about how the club was structured and financed. I was warned, in the nicest possible way, not to buy my beer in the clubhouse. 'Don't give him anything. He won't put it back into this club,' I was told. I didn't dare ask who 'he' was. On the way to the ground, Chester had introduced me to Dave. He was working in an Oxfam shop in central London. Dave was from Lincoln and had been following the Tons for just over a year. 'I don't know why,' he said. 'Maybe it's the history of the ground. Did you know it's London's oldest senior football ground? I've tried "proper" football but I'm hooked on this lot now. You feel a part of something exciting here.'

The history thing came up more than once. It was as if these guys and gals felt like they were custodians of something bigger than an east-end sports club. Clapton FC were founded more than 140 years ago, an amalgam of three teams who shared a pitch on Hackney Downs. In 1894 they were one of the founding members of the Southern League which in those days boasted membership of the likes of Millwall, Reading and Southampton. Located five miles north-east of the London dockyards, the club recruited players locally. Surrounded in all directions by some of the biggest names in the game, Clapton always had to fight their corner.

My game ended in a 3-1 defeat but the result counted for nothing. The season was to all intents over but the crowd went berserk anyway. The Tons' captain, Craig Greenwood, was carried shoulder-high towards the sacred Scaffold. He was beaming. Cue more flares, fists pumping the air, the throwing of beer and chanting. All the players stayed on the pitch for an impromptu end-of-season party. The manager, Chris Wood, made an impassioned speech. 'We can't pay these lads money,' he said. 'You know that. But you guys …'

'And girls,' came a shout from the back.

'Er, and girls,' he continued. 'Your support is brilliant. People have heard about you lot all the way up to the Ryman League. Please, please keep it up next season.'

* * *

The rhetoric I heard at the Old Spotted Dog that day in 2014 was not empty and the Ultras did finally take control of Clapton. Well, sort of. The fans had wanted to wrest the club from the owner for several years. They were unhappy with a lack of consultation with supporters, sudden ticket price hikes and overzealous security (they were banned from attending two away fixtures). There were accusations and counter claims and the Ultras ended up boycotting their own team. With guidance from Supporters Direct, a new team, Clapton Community Football Club, was voted into existence in February 2018.

The Clapton I saw, Clapton FC, is still going in the Essex League, still mid-table. Following their eviction from Forest Gate in 2019 the club now groundshares with Southend Manor at Southchurch Park in Southend-on-Sea. The new team, Clapton Community Football Club, meanwhile play in the Middlesex County League at Wadham Lodge. They may be way down the leagues and to all intents starting from scratch but they are always well supported on matchday. During the club's debut season Clapton Community sold more than 11,000 away shirts. In September 2019 it was confirmed that Clapton Community had been awarded the lease at the Old Spotted Dog.

The war of words between the old and new clubs, however, continued online. The 'official' Clapton FC website accused the Ultras of dissuading away supporters from watching them, of appropriating their traditional red and white strip and of misleading fans by using the name Clapton FC. It also countered what it said was misinformation from the newbies. The root cause of their differences was perhaps given away when the official club said, 'We have no political allegiances to any party either here in England or abroad. We respect the history of countries but are focused on the progression of football not politics.' So was it all about the politics?

The new club's website offers clear testimony of the Clapton Community's commitment to their guiding principles of inclusion and anti-fascism in east London. There is also a fascinating series of pen portraits of supporters. Gill Scott lives in Hull but says, 'I'm still an east London girl at heart. I went to school in Wanstead, just across the Flats. In Clapton I can be part of a club which not only has a wonderful ethos, but is truly run by the fans, for the fans, and is embedded in the community. "No pasaran", they shall not pass, the anti-fascist rallying call, is sadly more relevant today than ever. A club with the community engagement and the culture of Clapton is a very special thing and needs to be cherished. Our club is a shining light in what can be a very gloomy world.'

Another member, Annabel Staff, writes, 'CCFC provided the perfect antidote to modern commercialised football, which I had begun to grow very tired of. It all felt so disconnected, the corporatised club and the real fans being two completely separate entities, like modern football no longer needed fans in stadiums. Clapton is so far from this world and I think it's beautiful. The community is second to none, the fact that inclusivity is the core value of CCFC is what has made me truly become a lifelong fan. This is what football should be about – openness, community focussed support, anti-fascism, inclusivity, accessibility and of course pure, unabashed fun. It's fighting the good fight and I love it.'

Andy Barr first went to the Old Spotted Dog when he was 14 years old. 'There was something special about the ground. The old wooden clubhouse known as the "Upturned Boat", the local partisan support, despite their lowly league position, and the smoke-filled wooden shed that served as a committee room. This was a true amateur outfit, unfashionable at the time, but retaining the air of a proud, once-great football club.' Andy moved away but 11 years later, disillusioned by the professional game, he returned to Clapton and was once again hooked. He served 11 years as a committee member, secretary and vice-president. 'Whether one is new to the Clapton experience or, like me, one of the older supporters, this club still belongs to you and me. And, there is no football club like it.'

* * *

In July 2020 Clapton Community FC became the owners of the Old Spotted Dog Ground. Kevin Blowe from the club said, 'For the first time ever, the oldest senior football ground in London is owned by a football club, and a member-run, non-profit, community-focused football club at that. Finally having a ground of our own, owned by members, will offer long term stability for the club and also the chance to build lasting links with the local community.' Long live the east London revolution.

12

Kicking Off In North Korea

WHEN WE book a holiday, one of the first things I do is to check out the fixtures in the country we are travelling to. Different leagues play at different times of the year but there's almost always a game or a pre-season friendly to take in. I have managed to strike up conversations across the world solely through a shared passion for football. At a local match in Mauritius I was introduced to the island's international football officer. He had heard of Ryan Giggs and Gareth Bale of course while I knew nothing about Mauritian football. I do now. When I was there, all the grass pitches had been torn up to be replaced in time for a tournament for the islands of the Indian Ocean. Funds were tight, players undependable. For someone I had never met before we got on like a house on fire. On another holiday, in Cabo Verde, Helen and I celebrated Sporting Clube da Boa Vista's promotion to the national league with Mr Nando, the club's president. It was pure chance they were playing when we were on holiday, pure delight that they got promoted and we got to join the party.

So when Chester and I visited North Korea in 2013 there was one thing we just had to do. Chester was halfway through his gap year before university. I was chuffed that my boy still wanted to travel with his father rather than drink himself stupid in Magaluf. There are political flashpoints across the world which breeze in and out of the news. Every so often we are told the Iranians will soon have a nuclear device and that we should be scared. An Israeli-Palestinian crisis blows up every so often, seemingly never to be solved. And then we have North Korea or the Democratic People's Republic of Korea as they like to call themselves. The world's problem child maybe, but what a fascinating holiday destination.

Maybe it is the social realist architecture or the hammer and sickle symbols but Chester and I share a passion for post-communist societies. Over the years we travelled through eastern Europe, Russia and Cuba and arrived in the capital city Pyongyang fresh from Cambodia, Vietnam and China. This though, North Korea, was the real thing. 'Actually existing communism' to steal a phrase from the Brezhnev era. The reality of this socialist dream was both sobering and enlightening. I have recounted our trips to the gigantic monuments of the Korean leaders and to the nervy 'demilitarised zone' on the border with the South in my first book. But you may be particularly interested in our groundhopping experience in North Korea.

On our trip, day and night, we had three guides with us to mind a party of a dozen foreign visitors. Everything in the Democratic People's Republic was closely managed and controlled but we knew that's how it would be. Miss Kim and Mrs Kim spoke good English and were our main guides. They were not related. Kim is a very popular Korean surname. Bringing up the rear of the group was Mr Lim. We badgered Mrs Kim from day one. 'It would be really good to watch a football match while we are here. It's what we do in our country and I am sure the people of Korea all enjoy football just like we do.' I was trying to appeal to her national vanity, 'Here's an opportunity to show us the fatherland as a normal country. Show us a game and we'll go home and say you're regular guys, that you like the footie, just like the rest of us.' But of course Mrs Kim was working to a script set down by the ruling Workers' Party. There was nothing in it for her to deviate from the stage-managed visits to a collective farm and a hydroelectric power station. Innovation? Spontaneity? What was I thinking of? But amazingly, after two days, and after we had gathered a handful of our fellow travellers to the cause, she announced that we could indeed attend a match. Result.

You'll not hear Sky Sports presenter Jeff Stelling saying, 'There'll be dancing on the streets of Pyongyang,' any time soon. Because the North Koreans take their footie as seriously as their politics. That is to say, very seriously. This was the pariah country's match of the day – Pyongyang, the capital, versus Amrokgang, the army team. The game was a sell-out though you'd never have guessed it. As we entered the 50,000-seater Kim Il-Sung Stadium, the watchful eyes of the Eternal President and Great Leader and his son and heir Kim Jong-Il looked down at us from giant posters but there was no one else to be seen. There were no queues, no turnstiles and certainly no hot dog stands or programme sellers. Once inside it was a different matter. Every seat was taken. Row upon row of men dressed in identical dark suits and red ties sat silently. Each one of them sported a tiny enamel badge on their left breast. No, not the crest of Pyongyang FC, but of the Great Leader himself.

The artificial pitch looked immaculate under the spring morning sun. Kick-off was at 9.30am, but then it was a bank holiday and the match was to mark the 101st birthday of Kim Il-Sung. It was a strange sort of celebration. Maybe it was the early start but there were no chants, flags or scarves to be seen, just a quiet murmur around the stands, as if in anticipation. Some sections were reserved for soldiers who were all turned out in identical olive-green uniforms and broad-brimmed hats. I don't know if they were under orders to attend but some were quietly reading paperbacks and showed no interest in the game.

Amrokgang looked stronger in the first half though it was a scrappy match. The ball, which seemed to bounce and sway at the slightest touch, didn't help. Pyongyang fought back and won a penalty, though you would be hard-pressed to know that from the reaction of the crowd. There was none. Just silence. So we decided to inject some old-style British terrace atmosphere of our own and chanted, 'One-nil to the referee, 1-0 to the referee.' The visiting western tourists who had joined us in the VIP box (at €30 a seat – hard currency only please) laughed. They got the joke. That just made us bolder. 'Pyongyang ooh ooh! Pyongyang ooh ooh!' But the locals stared at us and I wondered if we had overstepped the line or had unwittingly caused offence. No one asked us to stop. We were just ignored. In a land where it seemed you must ask permission to speak, this show of individuality was not seen as rude or threatening. They stared blankly at us. I think they thought we were just a little odd.

Our every movement in North Korea had been strictly controlled. Miss Kim and Mrs Kim led us from the front and offered a slick commentary on all things North Korea while the mysterious Mr Lim rarely spoke. Was he minding us or making sure our guides kept to the script that all was rosy in this socialist utopia? We had only just made it into North Korea. The day before we arrived, the present leader, Kim Jung-Un, had threatened a nuclear attack on America. One of the borders with China was closed and we'd been checking the UK government's travel advice as best we could from Beijing. BBC World News would later report this game as an attempt by the country's leadership to show that it was 'business as usual' during these dangerous times.

'So the game's big here in Korea is it, Mr Lim?' I thought this would be the perfect ice-breaker. 'Yes. All men love it,' he said without breaking a smile. Success, I thought. At least he speaks. There are three leagues in North Korean football but because they play at different times of the year and because of the country's history of underhand international player transfers, these clubs cannot play in south Asian tournaments. There have been few moves abroad by players from North Korea, the notable exception being Han Kwang-Song who signed for Cagliari in Italy.

Han moved north to Juventus but did not play a single game in Turin. According to the Italian newspaper *Mundo Deportivo*, dealing with him was a nightmare as Kim Jong-Un himself acted as a shadowy father-come-agent figure controlling every aspect of the young player's career. In early 2020 there was talk of Han playing in the Premier League. Arsenal and Liverpool were rumoured to be interested. Nothing came of it and he now plays in Qatar. Nor are we likely to see Han or any other North Koreans playing in the Premier League. According to *The Sun*'s website, players who sign for a foreign team have to send their wages home to Pyongyang. United Nations resolutions ban North Korea from trading with any other countries and that could include remittances from abroad. Dr Udo Merkel from Brighton University says, 'Under current UN sanctions, money sent to the North Korean government would be seriously considered support for the nuclear programme for the country.'

The national side uses the official name of the country, the Democratic People's Republic of Korea (DPRK). They won't use 'North' because they say they are one country even though they have been technically at war with the South since the end of the civil war in 1953. The team is composed of both native North Koreans and Koreans born in Japan. The DPRK's greatest footballing moment came in the 1966 World Cup when they beat Italy 2-0 to reach the quarter-finals. They also qualified for the 2010 finals in South Africa. During that tournament, North Korea's coach, Kim Jong-Hun, told the media that he received 'regular tactical advice during matches' from Kim Jong-Il 'using mobile phones that are not visible to the naked eye' and which were purportedly developed by the Dear Leader himself. Of course.

Despite still being technically at war with each other, North met South Korea in Pyongyang in a World Cup qualifier in October 2019. Previous matches between these two countries had been held in the South or at a neutral venue. There was massive interest in the game but the DPRK authorities refused to allow any spectators into the stadium and the match was played in front of empty seats. No foreign media were allowed and the game was not broadcast on TV.

On the pitch it proved to be a bad-tempered affair with allegations of deliberate foul play. After the match the vice-president of the (South) Korea Football Association, Choi Young-il, said, 'It was like war ... They would use everything from elbows to hands to knees to fend off our players. It was really difficult. I have never seen something like this in football before.' His team's captain, Tottenham's Son Heung-min, was also surprised by the North's tactics. 'The match was very aggressive to a degree that I think it's a huge achievement just to return safely without being injured,' he said. So much for sport providing a soft diplomatic key to unlock the peninsula's problems.

Back on the pitch at our game, Amrokgang had got one back. Another penalty. Why the referee had to confer with the linesman, I don't know. The Pyongyang striker was taken down five yards inside the box. In fact the ref was having a nightmare, although you would not have known that from the reaction of the players and officials. The technical areas on the side of the pitch where coaching staff harangue the referee, the opposition and their own players were empty all game. Neither manager ventured out of the dugout nor was there any high-fiving or pats on the back when players were substituted. Now I like to watch controlled football, but not quite like this.

Amazingly, there was a riot at a football match here in 2005 in that same Kim Il-Sung Stadium, which was a sea of tranquillity for our visit. Soldiers and police had to step in as violence erupted as North Korea lost a World Cup qualifying match to Iran. Bottles, stones and chairs were thrown on to the pitch when a Korean player was sent off. The unrest continued after the final whistle and match officials were unable to leave the pitch for more than 20 minutes. Thousands of angry fans surrounded the stadium preventing the Iranian players from getting on their bus. It reportedly took two hours to disperse the crowd. 'The atmosphere on the pitch and outside the pitch was not a sports atmosphere,' Iran's coach Branko Ivanković said rather understatedly. 'It's very disappointing when you feel your life is not safe. My players tried to get to the bus after the game but it was not possible – it was a very dangerous situation.'

In an article in the *Los Angeles Times,* Andrei Lankov, a North Korea academic from Kookmin University in Seoul, wrote, 'If I were Kim Jong-Il, [the North Korean leader at the time] I would be quite terrified. If people can riot about football then they can as well about the food distribution or somebody's arrest. Something like this would have been unthinkable in Pyongyang ten years ago.' As it would be today, but Kim Jong-Un is still in power and the likelihood of the regime collapsing of its own accord seems as far away as ever.

Surprise, surprise, there was some half-time entertainment for us. A brass band piped up behind the goal. But immediately, as if they'd been waiting for their cue, another band behind the opposite goal struck up. They were playing different tunes. Were they bands from different sections of the armed forces competing against each other? Who knows? The match went into stoppage time as the fourth official held up a board showing two minutes. Pyongyang were pressing hard.

'Surely it's all over now?' said Chester, who was the only one still watching the game as if any of it mattered. The clock showed they had played for 94 minutes. At last the crowd seemed to rouse themselves, if only a little, at the prospect of a winning goal. I looked at my watch but the referee didn't look at his. Finally, Pyongyang scored with a low shot following some good inter-passing. It was the very last kick of the oddest game I have ever watched. Maybe the referee was under orders to ensure a home win on this special public holiday. But with no emotion one way or the other on the faces of the soldiers and party faithful as they marched silently out of the Kim Il-Sung Stadium, I simply couldn't tell.

13

Farewell 'Brian The Bluebird'

Brian Mertens was a founding member of the Cardiff City Supporters' Trust. He died at the age of 66 in 2018. Here is my tribute to a true football fan:

THERE'S ONE of them at every club in Britain, an individual or small group of people who are a permanent fixture on matchdays. It may be the old man with straggly hair you've seen chaining his bike to the railings for years, the woman who's been selling programmes from that booth since you started coming here or the family you've watched growing up at the players' entrance as they plead for autographs.

One such permanent at Cardiff City was Brian Mertens, 'Brian the Bluebird'. Come rain or shine, every matchday Brian would be standing with his walking stick outside the Supporters' Trust office just round the corner from Gate 5 at the Cardiff City Stadium. There he would recruit new members, sell raffle tickets or just chat to anyone who wanted to talk. With his long grey beard and thick glasses, he was recognised by everyone. The police, stewards and of course fans would shout a hello as they made their way past him into the ground.

Brian was a stalwart of the Cardiff City Supporters' Trust and had served on its board since its inception. He was our 'liaison officer' and would invite members from trusts of opposition teams to come and meet us before games. Through his work we made many new friends as we stood outside the office sharing advice and badmouthing the club's management with supporters from across the leagues. Didn't we all seem to have the same problems. Despite his long illness, Brian worked tirelessly to improve the game for the fans. A better example of creating friendship through football you could not have hoped to meet.

We would drive to Birmingham or to London together to attend the 'Supporters' Summit' or to meet with other trusts. All the way up the M4 Brian would excitedly discuss the City's latest hopeless season, Wales's prospects at the European Championship or which player we should bin next. In fact we got so animated once that we took the wrong turning on the ring road, got lost and missed the meeting altogether.

Well-informed and passionate in his beliefs, Brian was great company as well as being a good friend. He believed in the principles of fan representation at all levels and was determined to hold the club and the game to account for the benefit of us all. Thanks Brian for everything you did for our trust, for Cardiff City and for the supporter movement. We will miss you.

14

Mas Que Un Juego?

WHATEVER THE media may tell us, the Premier League is not the be-all and end-all of European football. Many top players believe they have not really proved themselves unless they have played 'abroad'. Italy and Spain would be the standout countries for such a move, although it doesn't always work out for them. There is an apocryphal quote from Ian Rush that his time in Italy was 'like living in a foreign country'. That myth has been debunked. Apparently Kenny Dalglish was the mischievous source but as Rush honestly put it, playing in Italy 'means I can look back on my career and not wonder about what might have been'. Some 25 years later, when Gareth Bale signed for Real Madrid, he said, 'I remember family holidays when we used to go to Spain, and we'd bring back replica shirts of Real Madrid and pretend to be the players when we played in the park.'

Maybe it's the memories of sun, sand and sangria but Spanish football has a special place in the hearts of supporters as well as players. The very best footballers go there. It's glamorous and you always think of them as winners. From a dank English terrace on a November night, cupping a hot tea, there is something unattainable about it all. The term Galácticos was invented to describe the world-class players that Real Madrid started buying back in the 2000s. Think Luis Figo, Ronaldo and Robinho. In Barcelona there were Ronaldinho, Xavi and later Messi.

The game in Spain has been dominated by these two free-spending clubs. Nearly every year from 2005 to 2020 La Liga was won by either Barcelona or Real Madrid (the only other winner was Atlético Madrid in the 2013/2014 season). The most eagerly anticipated game in the league is the encounter between them, aptly named El Clásico. But this fixation with just two teams does Spanish football a disservice. Clubs there, including the two giants, have a communal identity which transcends the game itself. I visited two regions of Spain, the Basque country and Catalunya, to see if football there really is 'mas que un juego', more than a game.

My one and only visit to watch Barcelona was in 2014. They were playing Celta Vigo. 'Nah, I'll never get tickets,' I thought. I've left it too late. The game was that night. However, a quick word with Juliet at the hotel desk and within a couple of hours I had a ticket in my hand, for the cheap seats, in the gods, behind the goal. They even gave me a programme wrapped in plastic. A snip at €45. I unkindly thought of it as football tourism but then remembered that Barcelona is no ordinary team. Founded in 1899 by a group of Swiss, English and local footballers, the club has become a symbol of Catalan culture, pride and resistance. Its motto in the Catalan language is 'Més que un club', 'More than a club'.

Superlatives about Barça abound. It is the most successful Spanish team of all time and the best-attended club in the

*One Game,
Two Nations.
Tennis Borussia
Berlin v BSG
Chemie Leipzig.
Mommsenstadion,
22 August 2020.*

*Ein Kultclub.
TeBe's very own
Jack Black.*

*Football without fans,
anyone?*

Covid lockdown. Cardiff City 3 v Hull City 3. Cardiff City Stadium, 22 July 2020.

Football with some fans. A hot ticket – Bulgaria 0 v Wales 1. Vasil Levski National Stadium, Sofia, 14 October 2020.

Red Star over Hong Kong. HKFC at the Happy Valley.

Hong Kong FC v Kwun Tong, Happy Valley Stadium, 5 November 2017.

What price your national anthem? The not so Happy Valley.

Beautiful, beautiful chaos. The African Cup of Nations, Libreville, Gabon. Another footballing white elephant.

Street football, Libreville, Gabon.

Wales Supporters 3 v Croatia 5. Osijek – 8 June 2019.

Fathers and sons. Wales Supporters 3 v Russia Supporters 3. Toulouse, Euro 2016.

Wales Supporters 3 v Ukraine Supporters 3. Wales win on penalties.

Two of my footballing heroes. David O'Gorman (Wales Supporters captain) and Oleg Salenko (1994 World Cup Golden Boot). Kyiv, Ukraine 2017.

Not a hidden problem. Bulgarian supporters team manager. Lviv, Ukraine, 2010.

Offering advice to the former Wales manager Chris Coleman. He didn't take it!

*Sometimes antisocial, always antifascist.
The Clapton Ultras (courtesy of @ClaptonCFC)*

*Two fathers, two sons.
The Kim Il-Sung
Stadium, Pyongyang,
North Korea.*

Silent football North Korean style. Pyongyang v Amrokgang at the Kim Il-Sung Stadium, April 2013.

Kim Il-Sung's 101st birthday

All in order at the Kim Il-Sung Stadium, Pyongyang, North Korea.

Me with Brian 'The Bluebird' Mertens and other Cardiff City Supporters Trust members, Paul Corkrey and Keith Morgan at the annual Supporters Summit.

With Athletic Bilbao's Koikili in Sondika, Euskadi, April 2011.

No Team GB! Mexico v Wales at the MetLife Stadium, New Jersey. 27 May 2012.

world. Barcelona generated a record revenue of $959.3m between 2018 and 2019, overtaking Real Madrid, to make it football's biggest cash-generating club. Despite this, the supporters are said to own and operate Barcelona. The team is also known as the 'equip blaugrana' and its distinctive garnet and blue colours are worn across continents; there are more than 1,000 officially registered fan clubs around the world.

The animosity between Madrid and Barcelona, indeed between the Spanish state and the Catalan nation, runs deep. Real Madrid represents imperial Spain, Barcelona a seven and a half million-strong nation with its own language and culture which feels downtrodden and wants to break away. It also happens to be the wealthiest of Spain's autonomous communities. The club has always played a part in the city and the region's history. On 14 June 1925 the Barça crowd jeered the Spanish national anthem in a spontaneous protest against Miguel Primo de Rivera's dictatorship. The ground was closed for six months as a reprisal. During the Spanish Civil War, Barcelona players fought for the Republicans and after the fascists' victory the club was forced to remove the Catalan flag from its badge. Supporting the team was a clandestine way of showing your support for the political opposition.

I wondered if this was still the case today. The region has seen a referendum in favour of ceding from Spain declared illegal, elected members of the Parliament de Catalunya imprisoned and the violent dispersal of peaceful street protests. So is the Camp Nou still a hotbed of nationalist revolt? Despite its capacity of 99,354, the night I visited, the famous stadium was almost empty and looked a little sad.

Celta Vigo were hardly a big draw but this was Barcelona wasn't it?

We had been placed in the tourist section. Young Japanese girls were holding nylon Barcelona flags and taking photographs. Lots of photographs. How many of them had ever attended a football match before, I wondered. Had they not read the morning paper? The headline in *La Vanguardia*, the Catalan daily, was that the Spanish Constitutional Court in Madrid had ruled the January declaration of sovereignty by Catalan Parliament 'unconstitutional'. I was baffled at how the club saw itself as an expression of national identity while at the same time selling itself as a hugely successful international brand.

However many star players were on the field that night I am sorry to say that the game was a drab affair. Yes, Messi scored and yes, Barça won 3-0. Every so often the locals in the tier below me tried to inject some passion but there can't have been more than 50 of them. They clapped and chanted, banged a drum and every now and again raised Catalan flags. But it all felt just a little bit weak. As if to underscore my contempt for my fellow sporting day-trippers, the Japanese got up and left the ground with 20 minutes of play remaining. Those garnet and blue nylon scarves would now adorn the walls of student digs and the selfies beamed home via Facebook. I could see the responses: 'Awesome!', 'Great pics'. But what was it all for?

In this country we call them 'plastics', faux supporters who follow successful teams, usually from a considerable distance. Some may never actually see 'their' team play. The clubs themselves love the plastics. It is they who buy the scarves and club mugs and pay through the nose for stadium tours. They build the brand and are happy to pay for the privilege. Here in Barcelona though, I was confused. Wasn't this a fan-owned club offering a weekly homage to, well, Catalunya? Yes, I too had allowed myself to be processed. I'd been given the opportunity to be a small part of the Barça brand and just like those stupid students with their stupid scarves I'd grabbed it. It had been a fine night out and I am glad to have visited the Camp Nou. But football as tourism? No thank you.

On his Outside Write website Chris Lee has written in depth about the role of politics in football across the world. In his blog on Barcelona and the Catalonian question, he says that as Barça looks towards more lucrative overseas markets, just as is happening in Britain, some fans have drifted away in search of smaller clubs and a more intimate and authentic football experience. Lee quotes the Barcelona-based academic and author, Natxo Parra, who says, 'There are people who are leaving following Barça to go to other stadiums, similar to what happened to FC St. Pauli in Germany in the 1980s. They are going to the terraces at CE Júpiter, CE Europa and Sant Andreu – much smaller clubs than Barça. These are places with much closer connection with the local people. This is where people find the atmosphere they want – a connection with their political values, connection with the anti-fascist movement, enjoyment of football and sharing terraces with their comrades.'

I discussed my contempt for the modern game at the highest level and football tourism in particular with my good friend and fellow groundhopper David Collins. He's a well-travelled supporter and came to Barnet with me to complete my visits to the 92 Football League and Premier

League grounds. David has visited stadiums in Belgrade, Manchester, Spain and Northern Ireland – even when no games were taking place. He just wanted to see the ground, 'tick it off', I suppose. David did not share my disdain for the Barcelona plastics. 'Of course I'd prefer the Japanese to support Grampus 8 rather than Barça,' he said. 'Maybe they do. But is there really a difference between them taking selfies at the San Siro or the Camp Nou and you and me doing the same at Port Vale?'

Three years after my visit to Barcelona, the people of Catalunya voted overwhelmingly for independence. What would have happened to the new nation's top football club had secession gone ahead? The president of La Liga said that he would not allow Barcelona to play in the Spanish league. Forget El Clásico, the big money and the world's best players, Catalunya's sport minister at the time, Gerard Figueras, saw this rejection not as a threat but as an opportunity. He proclaimed that Barça would be free to join another country's football league. The same would be true for the other two major football clubs in the north-east Spanish region. 'In the case of independence, Catalan teams in La Liga – Barcelona, Espanyol and Girona – will have to decide where they want to play: in the Spanish league or a neighbouring country like Italy, France or the Premier League,' Figueras said.

Of course it never came to pass. The Spanish state declared the independence referendum illegal and put the leaders of the 'insurrection' on trial. In October 2019, Spain's Supreme Court sentenced nine Catalan separatist leaders to between nine and 13 years in prison for sedition. FC Barcelona had backed the referendum and following the jailings it issued a measured and conciliatory statement: 'The resolution of the conflict that Catalunya is experiencing is exclusively through political dialogue. Therefore, now more than ever, the club asks all policy makers to lead a process of dialogue and negotiation to resolve this conflict, which should also allow the release of convicted civic and political leaders. FC Barcelona also expresses all its support and solidarity to the families of those who are deprived of their freedom.' Can you see Manchester United issuing a statement supporting the release of political prisoners in this country?

Locking up the region's leaders hasn't put an end to the matter. Until the Covid pandemic struck, street protests continued across Catalunya. The Clásico of October 2019 was cancelled due to the demonstrations. The rearranged match in December of that year saw thousands of police and security personnel deployed to the Camp Nou. Supporters of independence were keen to exploit the popularity and visibility of one of the world's most-watched football games. The afternoon of the match thousands of supporters of the 'Democratic Tsunami' group gathered near the stadium. Inside and outside slogans were chanted and, unlike my visit, the stadium was a sea of red, yellow and blue. The message on many banners read, 'Spain, sit and talk.'

Some 450km north-west of Barcelona lies the city of Bilbao in the Basque Country. In 2009 I travelled there to meet Koikili Lertxundi del Campo who was then playing for Athletic Bilbao. His team had just lost 2-0 to Sevilla. Most players would have been at home relaxing or loosening off in a swimming pool the day after a game. Not Koikili. He was hard at work at his second job. Koikili and his father Jabier run a consultancy which trains football coaches exclusively through the medium of Euskera, the Basque language. For years in Cardiff I had been coaching children in Welsh. Both languages are in a minority in their own countries and I wanted to see how the game could offer children an 'in' to a language which, by being associated with school, was just not cool to them.

More than half a million people speak Euskera across the northern-most provinces of Spain and into France. Following decades of decline, the language is making something of a comeback. It's not related to any other language and, with its juxtaposition of the letters X, Z and K, it must be a Scrabble players' dream. Or nightmare. The Basque 'region' is a passionately nationalistic country. When I visited, the ETA terrorist group, which had been fighting for full political independence, had only recently put down its arms. Koikili's dad Jabier was arrested in 1987, tortured, and sentenced to 12 years in prison for allegedly helping members of ETA escape from custody. Now the people of the Basque Country are seeking self-determination through purely democratic means. The culture is cherished and supported by most people, regardless of which language they speak. The parallels with Wales and the Welsh language were clear.

Koikili explained how children don't get the chance to speak Basque outside school. His mission is to train a new breed of coaches who make it the first language of play in this football-obsessed nation. In my faltering Spanish I asked how many of his fellow professionals at Athletic Bilbao had second jobs like this. Koikili answered in Basque through our friend Josu. 'None,' he said, 'but they are happy to give up some of their time to help us.' His club is supportive too, providing balls and bibs for the training sessions.

Athletic Bilbao is an interesting club. Migrant workers from England, Southampton and Sunderland in particular, were drawn to the iron mines and shipyards in the area. Along with their expertise, these men brought with them their love of football. Athletic Bilbao was founded in 1903 and retains the English spelling of its name – 'Athletic'. In 1909 a student called Juan Elorduy picked up 50 shirts in Southampton before catching the ship home and brought them to Bilbao. The colours are the same as the city's flag and the club started using its now-familiar red and white-striped strip in 1910.

Like Yorkshire County Cricket Club, the club used to only recruit players from its own region. Their favourite saying, and I have to quote it in Spanish here, is 'Con cantera y aficion, no hace falta importacion.' (With home-grown talent and local support, you don't need foreigners.) I can't see Cardiff City surviving long in football's pyramid if they ever followed a similar policy, but that was the only lesson from Bilbao that I chose to forget.

Koikili and I drove 20 minutes out of town to a training ground at the village of Sondika. This local club runs eight football teams across all age groups. As we arrived, two groups of 12-year-olds were being put through their paces. 'Kaixo, kaixo,' said Koikili, greeting everyone in Basque. We were there to watch a coach assessment session. The checklist was familiar to me: preparation, technique, feedback to players, any questions? But top of Koikili's list was the use of the Basque language by the coaches and how the children responded. It was no surprise that they all passed with flying colours.

By the last count 751,000 people, 28 per cent of all Basque territory (that includes all lands in France as well as in Spain), speak the language. It is widely used in education, the media and commerce, and with government support those numbers continue to rise. More importantly over 70 per cent of Basques under the age of 25 speak Euskera. A quarter of a century ago it was just 25 per cent. You can argue, and my experience in Wales bears this out, that the use of the language as an everyday common tongue is much lower than these figures suggest. The fear is that everyone will have some grasp of the native language while few will actually use it at home, in work or on the playing field. At the current rate of increase, however, on paper at least, Basque looks like it will soon be a majority language. Koikili told me that football was an important part of the rebirth of Euskera: 'The children can see that Basque belongs to them all and actually offers them an advantage on the pitch. It gives them that extra strength. It's a unique and powerful bond.'

In 2014, at the age of 33, Koikili Lertxundi del Campo retired from the professional game. After the appointment of the new Athletic manager, Marcelo Bielsa, he was deemed surplus to requirements. Koikili did go on to play for two seasons at Club Deportivo Mirandés in the Segunda División and his coaching work through the medium of Euskera of course continues.

There is, sadly, still some prejudice against Euskera. As recently as 2018 Basque footballers were told they could be sent off for speaking their own language during a game.

The match between Elgoibar and Idiazabal in the fifth tier of Spanish football was played in the Basque Country. The referee did not speak Basque and did not want 'to miss players using insults'. The Basque Culture and Sports deputy, Denis Itxaso, demanded an explanation. 'The attitude of this referee can't be overlooked,' he said. 'These types of episodes do nothing but create a lack of respect towards the language and heritage.' Unsurprisingly perhaps, the local council said no action would be taken against the official.

This incident made me wonder again about football, identity and nationhood. The reaction of police to non-violent protests, the jailing of elected politicians and the pettiness of a local referee show how tight a grip the Spanish state keeps on its autonomous regions. And yet FC Barcelona still acts as a rallying point for separatist sentiment as does Athletic Bilbao. These teams, and there are many others like them in Spain, serve a purpose beyond football. They are also expressions of deep cultural differences within a single nation state.

I looked at our situation here at home. Wales, England, Scotland and Northern Ireland all compete at international level in their own right and are wholly independent members of the governing bodies of the game, UEFA and FIFA. Why don't the Basque Country and Catalunya set up their own national teams in the same way the UK has done, thus having more than one 'home nation'? It would not necessarily mean the big teams get kicked out of a La Liga. There are many club/national league anomalies across Europe. Swansea and Newport play in 'foreign' English leagues. Monaco play in France and the Liechtenstein teams play in Switzerland.

Could a Basque and Catalan football team be a non-threatening focal point for national identity? There were discussions of a wholly Basque side as early as 1908 and something of the sort came together during the Spanish Civil War. It was called the Selección de Euskadi. Maybe the 'representative' element of the original name Selección was supposed to make it more palatable to the authorities of the unitary state of Spain. It was not until 1979, however, four years after the death of General Franco, that the Basque 'national' team began playing regularly again.

Their first match was a testimonial played for the benefit of the Basque player José Eulogio Gárate. Games were erratic but those first few matches of the Selección de Euskadi were played in support of a campaign to promote the Basque language and the gate receipts helped pay for 'ikastolas', the Basque language schools. After 36 years where Franco had banned any public display of 'Basqueness' this was for many a welcome re-appropriation of their own culture and identity. As Liz Crolley and David Hand note in their comprehensive study 'Football and European Identity: Historical Narratives through the Press', sport helped re-vindicate the Basque language. Koikili's coaching schools then are part of a long tradition whereby sport and particularly football is used to promote a much-cherished but endangered language.

From the early 1990s the Basque team began playing regular friendly matches, usually during La Liga's Christmas break. This reformed national team was part of a wider cultural and, for many, political resurgence. In 2006, Wales played a Basque XI at the San Mamés Stadium in Bilbao. The Welsh manager that night was one John Toshack, revered in the Basque Country thanks to his time as the manager of

Real Sociedad, who play in Donostia (San Sebastián). Wales won that game 1-0 thanks to a goal by Ryan Giggs. Recent matches have been played against Venezuela and Panama.

In December 2020 the Basque Football Federation applied to FIFA and UEFA to be officially recognised so that it can compete as a nation in international competition. The federation's lawyer, David Salinas-Armendariz, said the request represented 'the majority desire of Basque society', adding that joining UEFA and FIFA was 'a legitimate and absolutely viable objective from a legal point of view'. He cited the examples of the UK teams and said that European territories that were not independent states had been recognised before. In 1988 the Faroe Islands became an autonomous country within the Kingdom of Denmark, joining FIFA and, two years later, UEFA. By 2016 and despite objections from Spain, Gibraltar had been admitted to both international federations following a judgment of the International Court of Arbitration for Sport. Amazingly, Spain's prime minister, Pedro Sánchez, gave his support to the request of the Basque Football Federation. How the president of the Spanish FA feels about the prospect of losing Basque and then potentially Catalan players to his teams is of course another factor, and probably the deciding one.

15

No Team GB!

NEW JERSEY'S MetLife Stadium is hardly the place you would expect to see a political protest, least of all at a soccer match. But, thanks to the commitment and cunning of a few loyal supporters, that's just what happened when Wales played Mexico in the New York heat at the end of May 2012. This was a friendly international, Chris Coleman's first game as manager, and 2012 was the year of the London Olympic Games.

Wales, Scotland, Northern Ireland and England, the UK's four home nations, may compete as independent football teams but their athletes come together as Team GB every four years for the Olympics. However, as the Games were being held in London the English FA had the bright idea of also fielding a men's football team in the name of Great Britain. That combined team would play for the first time since the 1960 Games. To the armchair supporter, this Team GB may not have seemed a big deal, but to thousands of Welsh, Scots and Northern Ireland fans its very conception was a form of betrayal.

You see, we pride ourselves on our support for our *national* team. The Football Association of Wales was established in 1876. Our team has had its ups and mostly downs over the years but our support is ferocious and, wherever they play, a hardcore of us follow them. From week to week we may support Newport County, Llanelli or Rhyl. Your football club may choose many of the people you socialise with. Its fortunes too will often dictate your mood. But above your club comes your national team and for small countries like Scotland and Wales your affinity with your national team is an even bigger part of your identity. We have our own languages, history and traditions. I have not seen any backlash to Team GB coming from the dominant culture of Big Brother England. At no little expense we have watched Wales play all over Europe and beyond. So, betraying our devotion to 11 red shirts in the name of some footballing union that has never existed was a real slap in the face.

Back in New Jersey, Geraint, one of our biggest fans, physically as well as emotionally, had wrapped a hand-painted banner around himself and smuggled it into the ground. During the anthems my son and I helped him unfurl it. 'No Team GB' was the simple but defiant message. Craig Bellamy, the Wales captain who has a tattoo of the mediaeval Welsh freedom fighter Owain Glyndwr on his arm, had opted to be a member of Team GB that summer. When he saw the banner he ran across the pitch towards us. Very animated, he gestured at us to take the flag down, and from my lip reading, he wasn't too pleased at our message. But some things, Craig, are non-negotiable and my, our, football team is one such thing.

Team GB for the London Olympics was supposed to be a one-off. 'Calm down,' we were told, 'it won't happen again.' The team Craig and his mainly English pals joined crashed out in the quarter-finals of the Olympics and there was no such team in the Rio Games four years later. That you might have thought was that. But roll on six years and I began feeling like Bill Murray in the film *Groundhog Day*, where the hapless weatherman relives the same day, every day.

Football's world governing body FIFA announced that it had received written confirmation from the four home nations, yes, those same home nations who for more than 100 years have each been fielding their own independent football teams, that they were happy to field a women's Team GB for the Tokyo Olympics in 2020. Talk about turkeys voting for Christmas. Here we go again, I thought.

So, what are the objections to this one-off (well, now once every four years) coming together of the best men and women players in the United Kingdom? Quite a lot actually. Firstly, Team GB would not be entered at all unless the England women's team finished in the top three of the 2019 FIFA World Cup. They achieved that, but where did that leave the Scottish women's team who had also qualified for the finals in France? Even if the Scots had won the cup and England failed, there would be no Team GB. That seems a tad unfair. And if it did come to pass, who would select Team GB? Who would the manager be? That's right. It would have been in the gift of the England women's manager and the whole shebang run under the auspices of the English FA. Realistically, apart from Jess Fishlock and Sophie Ingle, no other Welsh women could have hoped to have got a look in. Team GB? Team England with a token Welsh or Scottish woman thrown in, more like.

However, the arguments over the practicalities of an Olympic team for an Olympics which did not go ahead are a side issue. Who gets to select the team and who gets to play are unimportant in the wider scheme of things. There is a matter of principle at stake here because there are plenty within the footballing family who resent the fact that the UK has four teams entered into international competitions, four votes within UEFA and FIFA and that every one of the home nations are custodians of the game's rules. They argue that a single team and a single association would free up more opportunities and greater influence to other, smaller nations in places where the game is growing, like Africa.

Their argument runs like this – if a single British women's team is deemed good enough for the Olympics, why not have a single men's team too? And if a united Team GB is acceptable in the Olympics then why not also field it for the World Cup and the European Championships? Farewell the four home nations. Without independent football teams you would not need four different national associations. Logically you would not need a Welsh or Scottish Premier League. Celtic and Rangers could try their luck in the English Premier League. The better Welsh teams too could also have a shot at playing over the border. It's a nightmare scenario but I fear that playing with Team GB is playing with fire.

Am I scaremongering? There is a risk if not an obvious threat. This is what Sepp Blatter, the FIFA president, said in 2008, 'If you start to put together a combined team for the Olympic Games, the question will automatically come up that there are four different associations so how can they play in one team. If this is the case then why the hell do they have four associations and four votes and their own vice-presidency [of FIFA]? This will put into question all the privileges that the British associations have been given by the Congress in 1946.'

It's often said with some pride that there are more members of FIFA than of the United Nations (the figure is 211 v 193). Membership of both continues to grow because the number of independent nations has grown in the last 40 years. This brings in new nation players who may not like the old rules. They will, however, all agree on the importance of international exposure through sport. Professor Martin Johnes of Swansea University has written for more than two decades about sport and national identity, including about the potential threat of a Team GB. He points to two previous threats to the UK's privileged position in world football.

In 1972 he says Uruguay withdrew a proposal to end the home nations' independence after they agreed to pay FIFA a levy from the British International Championship, which until then they had not been doing. It was also said at the time that the South American Confederation wished to remove the independence of the four associations. Fast forward to 1992 where the British delegates at the International Football Association Board, which writes the laws of the game, were told that if they voted against the introduction of the back-pass rule it would jeopardise their separate status. The formation of the League of Wales that same year was in no small part an attempt to underline the independence of the Welsh footballing territory.

FIFA defines a country as 'an independent state recognised by the international community'. None of the home nations, including England, is that. It would take just a handful of members to join together to get the issue on to the federation's agenda. The Confederation of African Football or CAF has 54 members. UEFA has 55. Africa gets to send five teams to the World Cup finals. There will be 13 European teams in Qatar. Why on earth would Comoros, Djibouti and Rwanda care about the plight of the pampered Brits?

What about the players though? Don't they deserve to play at the highest level? In case you forgot, the FIFA World Cup, for men and women, is the highest level. And if two professional players had to miss out on a month-long festival in Tokyo to save the international integrity of a team I have supported all my life, then so be it. When anyone is called up to play for their country they say they are humbled and that this is the highest honour in the game. Let's not dilute that honour by being part of a makeshift team which has no emotional appeal to the true football tribes of Britain.

Laura McAllister captained her country and played 24 times for Wales. Writing in the *Western Mail* she said that in her day football at the Olympics was simply not on their radar but that if she'd been offered a chance to play for a Team GB her answer would have been 'a very firm no'. Laura believes that playing for your country should be treated with the utmost respect. 'Lining up in the red of Wales and listening to "Hen Wlad Fy Nhadau" was as significant to me as the personal sporting recognition that came from making the team,' she said. 'It is something visceral and, therefore, almost impossible to quantify or articulate. The emotion and passion of international sport is what makes it so uniquely special and it's my view that this emotion is indivisible.'

The argument over Team GB again raises the big unspoken question – who is professional football for? For the benefit of a handful of players and agents and sponsors? For the aggrandisement of officials and their patrons? Or for us the supporters who part with our money and share our passion as part of a team we can truly call our own? It is, at heart, a matter of identity. I don't think my English friends, who are part of a cultural, political and sporting majority in the UK, quite understand what supporting a team like Wales means.

In his article 'Eighty Minute Patriots? National Identity and Sport in Modern Wales', Martin Johnes quotes fellow social historian Eric Hobsbawm, 'The imagined community of millions seems more real as a team of 11 named players.' The 80 minutes in Johnes's title refer to the length of a rugby match, traditionally but erroneously, believed to be the national sport of Wales.

Johnes has done a better job than I of crystallising what supporting your national team means. He says, 'For nations without a state, ethnic basis or even linguistic unity, the team of 11, or even 15, people takes on added significance. For many people in the so-called Celtic fringes of Britain, it is one of the few pieces of tangible evidence that their nation exists.' He argues that sport has acted as a key to imagined communities and that it is 'more real and accessible than any vague notion of a common history inheritance'.

At the end of August 2018 I joined a packed house at Newport's Rodney Parade stadium to see the Welsh women take on England. At stake was a place in the World Cup finals. The papers described it as 'the biggest day in Welsh women's football'. History was in the making. 'Get behind the girls,' they said. It was a great evening out. Young girls got to see their role models in action and we sang our hearts out for the nation. Wales went down 3-0 as we the Welsh said au revoir to our French World Cup dream. But hey, we'd given it a go. So, what should I now do with all that passion? Pack it away along with the Red Dragon flag, unfurl the Union Jack and move my allegiances to Team GB? Not on your life!

In the event, the Covid pandemic put paid to the Tokyo Olympic Games and the issue of Team GB was on hold. But like some monster waking from a deep slumber you can bet it will be back to haunt us again sometime soon. Now where did I put that banner?

16

First Clear The Goats

WHEN I managed my lad's under-13s football team, the first thing I had to do was to clear the pitch of dog muck. In Gambia they clear the pitch of goats, not their muck, but the animals themselves, extended families of which seem to have the freedom to roam at will. Welcome to Serrekunda East Park. Just a few kilometres outside the capital city Banjul, it's a stadium, of sorts, with just a small concrete stand running half the length of one side of the pitch. East Park is home to a number of local teams including the wonderfully named Steve Biko FC (Biko was a young South African anti-apartheid campaigner who was beaten to death by security forces in 1977).

As I arrived, the players were warming up, shrouded by clouds of dust which puffed up around them every time the ball hit the ground. I paid the princely sum of 25 local dalasi, about 30p, for the privilege of sitting under the afternoon sun on bare but thankfully cold concrete. The cordoned-off VIP section had a few rows of plastic garden chairs laid out in loose rows. 'Who's who?' I asked my new footballing friend Mordour, pointing at the teams. 'Not sure. Banjul in blue maybe,' he said nonchalantly, 'but that guy's a big deal.' Mordour gestured not towards the pitch but at the posh plastic seats next to us. A tall man looking relaxed in an open-necked shirt smiled as he greeted everyone with big handshakes. 'He's the local mayor. A very generous man.' Nice touch, I thought. 'Man of the people' supporting his local team.

Today's match of the day was supposed to be the Armed Forces against Banjul United in the Gambian League First Division. A regular league match. That's what I had been told. That's what I was expecting. And it was what was written on the league's website. The presence of the mayor and his beefy security guard, the singing of the national anthem, and the lengthy introduction of Mr Big to both teams should have told me something else, that this was not the top of the table clash I was expecting.

I should also have guessed that you don't travel to the smallest country on mainland Africa for the quality of the football. The standard was that of a poor Welsh third-tier match, which was odd given that the warm-up by both teams had been professional. The game itself saw the white shirts put in a few hefty tackles but the play was low on skill with long, directionless balls ending in a pointless race to the touchline. To call it 'industrial' would have been to presume some sort of game plan. I should have felt at home: it was a little like watching my Cardiff City play but without the occasional long shot on goal.

I asked Mordour about the game in Gambia. He thought for a little while and then asked me if I'd seen a group of Belgians in my hotel. I had noticed six middle-aged men drinking together by the pool speaking French and thought it a bit odd. The Gambia is not exactly the place for a 50th birthday party or a stag weekend. 'They're scouts looking for new and cheap talent,' he said. 'Anyone who's any good here goes straight to Senegal and from there, who knows? France, Belgium maybe. It's a way out and every footballer here dreams of it.' There was no anger in Mordour's eyes. He was probably thinking 'good luck to them'.

I had read about African players being promised untold riches by foreign football agents. The phrase 'football slavery' was coined to describe those unfortunate young men who ended up stranded many miles from their homeland and living in poor conditions. A few years earlier, Sepp Blatter, the head of FIFA, had criticised Europe's richest clubs for the way they scour the developing world for talent. In a column quoted by the BBC he said, 'I find it unhealthy, if not despicable, for rich clubs to send scouts shopping in Africa, South America and Asia to "buy" the most promising players there.' He added, 'Europe's leading clubs conduct themselves increasingly as neo-colonialists who don't give a damn about heritage and culture, but engage in social and economic rape by robbing the developing world of its best players.' And in a footballing footnote which would be delicious if it were not so ironic, Blatter concluded, 'If we're not careful, football may degenerate into a game of greed – a trend I will vigorously oppose.'

Really? In late 2020, FIFA filed a criminal complaint against Blatter over the finances of its loss-making football museum in Zurich. A carefully worded statement said that its former management 'repeatedly misled different FIFA bodies as to the cost and viability of the project' and that it suspected nepotism in relation to the project. In March 2021, following its own investigation, FIFA gave Blatter a new six-year ban from football and fined him one million Swiss francs. The organisation's ethics committee found that he had abused his position of trust and had breached rules regarding conflicts of interest and of offering or accepting gifts or other benefits.

The export of any half-decent players from Africa went some way to explaining the quality of the fare I was watching that afternoon in Serrekunda. It also said a lot about the economy of this little country. Not that any of this mattered because the spectacle in Gambian football for me was not on the pitch but all around you, right there in the stand. It was a riot of colour and sound. From kick-off to the final whistle there was a cacophony of music which didn't let up. One man banged a drum which somehow sounded a double beat. A lone saxophone added a simple riff in a rhythmic loop while almost everyone in the crowd slapped two pieces of wood together blasting out a wall of sound.

The whole show was orchestrated by a group of women who shook and danced on the dusty walkway in front of the stand. Every so often two lads would run out from the crowd and do an asymmetric dance-come-kung-fu move in what looked like a tribal dance. They would clap hands and laugh before disappearing back into the stand as everyone roared their approval. One big woman then rolled out to the front and shook her ample self to the beat. Groups of little children squealed and hit their sticks. I seemed to be the only one taking any interest in the game. The beat went round and round me in the afternoon heat.

Older women, oblivious to this mayhem, threaded their way through the crowd with pans balanced on their heads, their hands free to reach up and serve you. For a few dalasi you could get a polythene bag of water or a twist of ground nuts. Mordour waved to one of the women and handed me a small orange which she sliced open. He laughed as I slurped the juice up through the hole she had just cut. Shaven-headed kids and dreadlocked teenagers, Muslim girls with their heads covered, others wearing baseball hats, were all enjoying their day out. Young and old stood, danced and shouted together. So this is what they mean by family-friendly football.

The music did stop at the final whistle of the most glorious, low-quality, goalless draw I have witnessed. The football had been secondary to having a good day out. As the sun finally dipped, shaking off the worst of the heat, we stood behind the goal chatting. Mordour introduced me to a referee friend of his. We spoke about football in Africa and whether the fourth official should have been interfering with the assistant's decisions over more than one contested throw-in. The referee said 'yes', but I thought it was not in the laws of the game.

I took one last look at the stadium. 'Er, why are the players still on the pitch?' I asked. 'It's gone straight to penalties,' said the ref. But this was a bog-standard league game wasn't it? Nope. This was not the Armed Forces versus Banjul United but a local cup final, and Mr Mayor was the guest of honour. I looked at Mordour questioningly. He shrugged his shoulders and we both laughed. I later found out that I had watched Rangers FC beat Zurich 4-2 on penalties. Oh well, at least I got to see some goals.

17

Hope Reigns Supreme

THE CIVIL Service Sports Club just off the M4 motorway is an unlikely training ground for your national team. But Wales's homeless players were showing just as much passion as any European or South American superstar as they were put through their footballing paces. The competition was strong as the tackles came flying in fast and hard. At stake was a place to represent your country in the starting line-up at the 17th Homeless World Cup finals.

Players from more than 50 countries had travelled to the Welsh capital, Cardiff, to play in the week-long festival of football. The tournament helps transform the lives of people experiencing homelessness and since the first competition in Austria in 2003 the finals have been played in Mexico, Norway, Scotland and Chile. When I met the Welsh players and coaches there was no doubt in their minds how re-engaging with the game of football had proved to be life-changing.

Dai was 42 years old and had been in and out of prison since he was 15. He was thick-set, had a shaven head and still looked like the no-nonsense centre-half he was in his prime. Dai started taking drugs as a youth and ended up dealing on the streets of the steel town of Port Talbot. He said, 'I played a bit of football back then, had a job for a few months but it was all getting out of control.' Dai got sacked and made a living out of selling drugs to fund his own habit.

'I ended up shooting someone,' he said and turned away from me. I turned away too. This was his story and I wanted him to tell it, but in his own time. There was a pause. 'Okay, the person didn't die,' he finally said, 'but I think about it every day. I regret it every day.' Four years ago Dai's brother died. It was time to change. 'It was the first time I saw my mother cry,' he said. 'It's hard to explain. I started volunteering with the street football crowd and somehow it all came together.'

The crowd Dai hooked up with is called Street Football Wales, an organisation which promotes social inclusion in disadvantaged communities. It uses the game to bring together young people who may be homeless, have mental health issues or who are going through the criminal justice system. Dai leaned back on the bench we were sitting on as we watched the hopeful players trudge off the pitch. 'I sort of knew I'd taken from the system all my life,' he said. 'It was time to give something back.' Dai returned to playing and was part of the homeless team which represented Wales in the Oslo World Cup in 2017. He is now helping coach the current Welsh team.

Four thousand miles away in Minneapolis, Minnesota, a player who calls himself 'A' had a similar story. 'A' loved playing soccer but he too hit hard times and ended up on the streets. Looking for a place to stay, he found his way to a charity called YouthLink. There he met an outreach worker called Jose Acuna. That meeting changed his life. Acuna runs a street soccer team where homeless young people learn that football is more than just a game. Acuna says that through the contact and engagement he had off the pitch, 'A' was able to connect with a night shelter, somewhere for him to stay. 'He now has a place of his own,' Acuna said. 'He's a go-getter type of person and has worked very hard to achieve his goals not only on the field, but in life.'

'A' says that football saved him from loneliness and misery, 'It's just somewhere you get to feel like you're human again, where you're welcome, where your background has nothing to do with the sport itself.' 'A' was selected for the USA national team and, while travelling to Wales for the Homeless World Cup offered him a personal opportunity and challenge, he wants the wider messages, beyond football, about deprivation and isolation and their causes, to also be heard.

The tournament has separate competitions for men and women's teams and the games are played on specially constructed, smaller pitches. Teams come from as far afield as Zimbabwe, Ivory Coast, South Korea, Colombia and Cambodia. Mexico were defending their world title in both competitions at the Cardiff finals. It was difficult to know who the better teams were. There's no form to go by really as players only get to play in one World Cup. But, in a sense, winning is not the point.

There are only four players per team on the field at any one time. When you first watch one of these games it feels a little odd. Possession is everything and no one will go for goal unless they are absolutely certain that a clear shot is on. The rules are specific on who can and cannot play for a team: players must have been homeless or have been an asylum seeker within the previous year.

This year's tournament was held in the shadow of Cardiff Castle and its commanding Norman keep. Under the dark leaf canopy of Bute Park the site was a melee of people, colour and geniality. The games were well attended. There was a feelgood factor at work, as if everyone present – players, supporters, or the just plain curious – knew that this was a good thing to be a part of.

I stood in the shade of one of the great trees with Keri Harris, the Wales squad manager, as his players came off elated after another successful match. He used to work with *Big Issue,* the magazine which homeless people help write and then sell on the streets of UK towns and cities. Having been involved with street football for 16 years Keri knew all the players personally. He was at the very first Homeless World Cup in Graz, Austria. 'Things were different back then,' he said. 'Our last squad player was only selected the night before we left. I walked into the homeless hostel in Swansea and said, "Who's got a passport and can kick a ball?" His name was Fowler and he spent the whole week telling everyone he was Robbie Fowler's brother. He was a nice guy but couldn't play football to save his life. While we were out there in Austria he never once kicked a ball.'

Everyone here had a story to tell and needed little prompting to tell it. Zamu came from Uganda to Wales to flee persecution. 'I just wanted somewhere safe to stay, just move my life forward,' she said. 'I thought football would be something to help me, to create friends. I now have a community, a place where you are accepted. It makes me feel like I have a family.' Zamu played for Wales in the 2016 Homeless World Cup in Glasgow. She says, 'Playing football makes me happy. It makes me who I am. It helps me build my confidence in everyday things. I moved from being homeless to studying and then living on my own.'

While this World Cup is about turning lives around it's also about having fun, and everyone is welcome. Of the 500-plus players who took part in the 2019 Homeless World Cup, I think that Team Norway's Charlotte Fosser was the only grandmother I saw play. The 42-year-old has five children and also fronts a rock band in her home city of Stavanger. Her life has been marked by addiction, abuse, an abortion, suicide attempts as well as an attempt on her life by others. For Fosser, playing in the World Cup finals marked the end of a long road to redemption. 'It's been a hell of a trip,' she said. 'Meeting people from a lot of different countries and stuff like that. And it's been wonderful. Even though we lost a couple of games, we still had fun. This is something you get to do once in a lifetime. Who can say they have played in the world championships? It's amazing.'

It's estimated that 100 million people are homeless worldwide. The streets of that year's host city, Cardiff, with its tents and makeshift shelters along the main shopping streets showed that this is a problem for all nations. The organisers of the tournament in Wales were at pains to say that they wanted to create a legacy that would last long after the final whistle was blown. Alongside the football there was a music festival and a 'debate tent' where high-profile speakers discussed issues around inequality and injustice. The idea was to think up some innovative solutions.

The Hollywood-based – but still very much Welsh – actor and activist Michael Sheen led the bid to host the tournament in Cardiff. In the lead-up to the cup, he said, 'All around the world I've seen how football can play a massive part in helping people transform their lives, bring some joy and hope when things seem at their worst. The football pitch works best when we help each other out. It's the same in life. Hope reigns supreme at the Homeless World Cup.'

I got a chance to meet the man himself. Sheen was there to greet the players as they arrived a few days before the tournament kicked off. All the teams were staying in halls of residence at a university sports campus. Players in tracksuits spoke animatedly as bus after bus spilled them on to the car park tarmac. They looked around in the bright sunshine trying to take in the unfamiliar surroundings. With their lanyards and outsized identity cards swinging across their chests they seemed a little overawed, vulnerable even.

Sheen though looked stylishly dishevelled in a polo shirt and blue cotton jacket as the PR people brought him over to me. It was his umpteenth interview of the day but he was genuinely excited about the possibility of change. 'I didn't get it at first,' he said. 'I asked them, "Why are you doing football rather than dealing with the real issues?" But they are. They're using football to relate to people who are difficult to connect with. People who have been judged, who have a stigma. On the football field they're not being judged anymore. When they come on the pitch they let go of all their stress, their cares and this opens the door to give them the opportunities they deserve.'

Sheen was a bit of a footballer himself in his day. He was offered a trial for Arsenal when he was 12 but it was not to be. He still plays a few charity matches but when I asked him about the Welsh rivalry, Cardiff versus Swansea, he was unusually reticent. You see, Sheen's a Port Talbot boy and lying between Wales's two main cities the town has split loyalties. 'I want to see them both do well,' he said with a smile. Most diplomatic.

I'd been told in confidence by a friend that this World Cup was in real danger of not going ahead. A sponsor had pulled out and Sheen himself stepped in at the last minute to plug the funding gap. Later that week in a TV interview he spilled the beans. Yes, he had put a lot of money in to make it happen. 'But d'you know,' he said, 'I'm lucky that I can go back to work and make that money back up.'

My last question to Sheen was pretty blunt. 'What one thing do you want to come out of this World Cup?' 'Legacy,' he said, without hesitation. 'What I really want is that when homelessness does occur we make it brief, rare and non-recurring. Let's get more focus on preventative measures and stop "othering" people. We need to see this,' he gesticulated to the players lining up outside the sports hall to register, 'as our community.'

Michael went off to yet another interview and I stood on the sidelines as the Wales team finished their warm-down. The men and women went off to change and I led Mark Atkinson, the Wales team's goalkeeper, to a corner of the artificial pitch. We sat cross-legged on the AstroTurf, his shiny bald head and ginger beard framing a big smile. Looking back I see a certain irony in talking to an ex-prisoner inside a cage. But that fence in every sense was now behind Mark.

Rugby was his first love and kept him fit when he was a soldier in the Royal Regiment of Wales. But life after the Army can be cruel and Mark got into smoking spice and drinking alcohol, lots of alcohol. He ended up in prison but, during his rehab, the chaplain suggested having a kick-about with some of the other inmates. 'Nothing ventured, nothing gained, I thought,' said Mark. 'Since then I haven't looked back. Being around people that have been on similar paths to me, I just felt included again and I've met some amazing people.'

Mark described himself as a recovering alcoholic, and despite being sober for four years, he said football came round at the right time. 'I was getting a bit complacent with my rehab,' he said, 'but then being around other people who were not as far down the line as me, I said to myself, "Stop it. You're not fixed yet!"'

At 44, Mark was the oldest member of the Wales team and during a pre-tournament training camp in west Wales the players were asked to write and share a sentence about every one of their team-mates. It was a sort of group therapy. Mark stroked his beard and paused before telling me, 'One of them said I was a "daddy" figure and that they could talk to me about anything.'

As part of his recovery programme, Mark was asked to write a farewell letter to his drug of choice. He's framed the letter and hung it on the wall in his partner's house. 'It inspires me. Every morning I look at it. It's like a mantra that keeps me going.' Mark had a lot of help from Care After Combat and is now using his own experience to help others. When I met him he was looking forward to going back inside the following week, to Cardiff Prison, only this time to mentor other army veterans. 'I'll probably know most of them,' he joked. 'Look at me,' he said as we got up to leave the cage. 'Representing my country. In my home city. Yep. Life is pretty damned good at the moment.'

* * *

Postscript: Mexico won both the men's and women's 2019 Homeless World Cup.

18

Doing The 92

'WELCOME TO The Hive' read the garish black and amber sign set alongside a busy suburban road. To the uninitiated there's nothing special about Barnet Football Club in north London. But this was my Golden Fleece, my Emerald City at the end of a long and winding road. Because after a quarter of a century of traipsing across the country I was about to join a select band. The Hive was my final visit. The 92nd ground of the 92 clubs in the top four leagues of English football.

From Accrington Stanley's brilliantly named Wham stadium in Lancashire to the uber-modern opulence of Arsenal's Emirates, from Meadow Lane to Molineux, Valley Parade to Vicarage Road, I had watched a game of football in them all.

For the hardy fans who have visited every single ground and want to celebrate their achievement there is a club and a website. The 92 Club has even made up ties and badges for its select, self-selecting, membership. Roger Titford, a Reading fan, was one of the club's early members. He describes 'doing the 92' as 'the sticker album for grown-ups'.

My own quest started when I took my wife Helen and son Chester to Edgeley Park to watch Stockport County play. They're not even in the Football League now, that's how long I have been doing this malarkey. It was our first Cardiff City away-day as a family. We met up with old college friends after the match and got to see some of the north-west of England. That was it. I'd caught the ground-hopping bug and the one-off away-day with my club had kickstarted a lengthy and sometimes expensive quest.

Almost every other Saturday we would drive to an away match. We developed our own family game to while away the hours. It was really simple: how many football teams can you get on a single road sign? You would start with Cardiff and Newport on the M4. Okay, two is not many, but it was a start. The M5 northbound was more difficult as there is a gap between Kidderminster, Birmingham and Walsall. We weren't sure whether we could accept Aston for Aston Villa either. What a delight then the M6 proved to be with Liverpool, Manchester, Preston and Walsall disappearing over our heads in big letters. But has anyone beaten the M60 eastbound? Burnley, Bury, Leeds, Huddersfield and I think we got Oldham and Sheffield in there somehow. Our family record is six clubs on one sign. Beat that!

These sporting away-days became cultural days out as we added museums and galleries to our list of football grounds to be ticked off. On the way to Middlesbrough we followed Bram Stoker up the steps to Whitby Abbey and its marvellous Celtic cross. In the Manchester Art Gallery, Ford Madox Brown's *Work* prompted some interesting discussion about child labour, social change and what the Victorians ever did for us. Newcastle city centre at night, however, was a different kind of cultural experience for a young boy, as Chester was then.

As a family we visited almost every Norman cathedral in England, via football. There was Exeter, Norwich and Carlisle. We pored over St Chad's Gospel in Lichfield on the way back from Sheffield (United not Wednesday, you understand). We learned that the illuminated pages were originally known as St Teilo's Gospels and as a proud Welsh family we planned a daring raid to bring them back to their rightful home, Llandaff Cathedral, which as it happens is just at the end of our street. We were intrigued at the strange beasts painted on the mediaeval ceiling in Peterborough (how did they get up there to do that?). And in Winchester Cathedral on our way home from Southampton we pondered the significance of the Magna Carta and the meaning of citizens' rights. All these visits went some way to placating Chester's junior school head, Mrs Jones, especially when we both bunked off for a midweek match. 'It's not just about the 90 minutes on the pitch, miss, honest.'

Football of course has its own cathedrals – its stadiums. Archibald Leitch was the doyen of 20th-century stadium architecture, and one of his masterpieces, Craven Cottage, is still home to Fulham FC. He first built a pavilion, the present-day Cottage, and then the Stevenage Road Stand in his characteristic red-brick style. 'The Fulham Football Club' is painted in white letters on black across the side of the building.

As you make your way to the stand behind the Cottage you sense history and tradition, the great afternoons that

generations of families and friends have had cheering on
their idols at the Cottage. I can remember seeing George
Best and Bobby Moore on television playing here at the end
of their careers. Johnny Haynes played 658 times and scored
158 goals for Fulham between 1952 and 1970. No, I never
saw him play either, but that's not the point. Every team in
every town and city has its own heroes, its own 'cottages'.
These temples of football are as important to supporters as
cathedrals are to believers.

Between 1899 and 1939 Leitch built some 20 stadiums
including Anfield and Goodison Park in Liverpool, Preston's
Deepdale, and Bramall Lane and Hillsborough in Sheffield.
Each one of these grounds has its own footballing history
and folklore. In 2009, after 99 years, my own club Cardiff
City left the gorgeous, crumbling Ninian Park. We accepted
the inevitable and moved across the road into a gleaming
new construction of concrete and steel. The Cardiff City
Stadium does not have the charm or, as yet, the history of
the old ground, but it is ours and new memories, songs,
stories and traditions are being forged by fans here.

Football, 'doing the 92', has allowed me, obliged me, to
explore the whole country and visit stadiums old and new.
The game seems tailor-made for obsessive behaviour. Some
fans collect their ticket stubs. Chester has three old-style
photo albums full of coloured match tickets, and keepsakes
from across the footballing world. The Hartlepool one has
as a background a panoramic shot of its stadium in washed-
out colours. We first stood behind the goal at Victoria Road
in 2001. The Italy versus Wales ticket from Bologna 1999
shows a posterised scene of Azzurri players in action. It's
a miniature work of art. While Chester filled his albums

I pasted my tickets on to a large piece of cardboard and added a frame. Each one of these pictorial gems will rekindle memories and fire stories of good times. Andy Hurst from Newport County keeps them under the bed in shoe boxes and calls them his 'ticket porn'.

It would be easy to dismiss us groundhoppers as a little sad, anoraks, obsessives with nothing better to do with our Saturday afternoons and Tuesday evenings. But hold on, I don't own an anorak. You wouldn't call an opera buff who travels the world to catch the perfect rendition of *La traviata* an obsessive. I have actually had a long conversation along similar lines to those we have at the football with a music lover. 'Her Violetta was good in Milan but not a patch on last year's performance at the New York Met,' he said. This guy also collected programmes from every opera he had attended. 'Ah,' I hear you say. 'But that's a hobby.'

This round-Britain quest has been much more to me than ticking off football grounds. I make a point of talking to people on the way to, from and inside the ground. Hutch, a reformed hooligan in Sunderland, befriended us outside the Stadium of Light. 'I'll walk you all to the ground,' he said, 'just in case.' In Nottingham we met Andy and the following year we stayed with his family when we went to watch Forest. He shared his passion for music with us and we stood in awe at his impressive CD collection, from Schubert to Saint Saens, though Beethoven is his favourite. Another passion, another collector. We tied in a pre-Christmas visit to Lincoln City's Sincil Bank stadium with a glorious rendition of the Messiah in the cathedral. This then has been a social and cultural, as much as a sporting, journey.

Being football though there's always an argument over the rules of the game. Some members of the 92 Club expect you to note the opposition, attendance and date of every game you watch. My groundhopping pal David Collins opined, 'I've watched Arsenal youth play at the Emirates. Does that count?' Yes David, I think so. Goodness, at this rate they will expect us to produce match tickets and photographic evidence before we can join the club. Sad but true, for me that wouldn't be so difficult. By whichever rules you choose to play this game each one of us knows in his or her heart of hearts whether he has 'done the 92'. You can't cheat yourself.

So, what of my final curtain, the game at Barnet? There was a nice irony in the fact that when I visited the Bees they were 92nd out of all 92 teams, at rock bottom and in real danger of 'doing a Scarborough' and falling out of the football league altogether. It was a 'do or die' match against Notts County, whose main claim to fame is that they are the oldest football team in the league. They have since dropped to the fifth tier of the game. As the scrappy game at The Hive drew to its conclusion it was still 0-0. Then came a thunderbolt of a shot from Barnet's Alex Nicholls to seal it for the home side. The goal was timed at 92 minutes.

So, what shall I do with my Saturdays now that my collection of football grounds is complete? Well, Spurs have moved to a new stadium since I visited them, new teams are promoted from the National League every year and, of course, the Welsh leagues are already in my sights.

19

Floodlight Porn

IF YOU stood outside our old house in the late 1990s and looked left you could see the floodlights of Ninian Park, the home of Cardiff City FC. It wasn't really that far to the ground, just a few free kicks away across Cowbridge Road and down to Leckwith. I would look up at these rusting giants as I came home from work and make a mental note of the next home match when I would be sitting in their shadow. The lights kept watch over the hallowed turf even when there wasn't a game on. They offered me a form of comfort, of good things to come.

Back then I had a dream, or was it a recurring daydream, that I was watching *Football Focus* one Saturday lunchtime. The player profile started with a close-up of those Ninian Park lights. The camera panned down to my son Chester who in my dream was by then a teenager and had just signed for his hometown club. He was joking with Garth Crooks as they turned the corner of our street and walked through the open door of the little house at number 62 before sitting down for a chat. Of course the dream never came about.

We moved to another part of the city, Chester never became a professional footballer, the club built a new stadium and those glorious floodlights were torn down.

Old-school floodlights conjure up different times and these ungainly, functional and, dare I say it, ugly structures have an odd hold on my imagination. My attachment to the rusting Victorian skeletons grows stronger as more and more of them are taken down to be replaced by polished white lights embedded in the streamlined new stadiums.

I am not alone in my love of floodlights. There's a dedicated Twitter account called Floodlight Porn where people share pictures of their favourite lights. 'Dave the Photo' has shared his views from Southend United's Roots Hall. I remember a superb midweek match there, the rain swirling across the pitch, every droplet caught in the light, spraying my eyes with tiny flashes of white. It seems that only when the floodlights disappear do people start opining about their old but by then lost grounds. Swansea had a particularly impressive angular set of lights at the old Vetch Field which craned awkwardly over the stand behind the prison. It was like some space invader readying itself to march on to the pitch. Wolves' ground, Molineux, was spectacular before it too was redeveloped. The lights there bookended a massive stepped terrace below a corrugated roof, the crash barriers all painted yellow. Football like it used to be. Or how we imagined it.

Sheffield's Bramall Lane lays claim to have been the first ground to have hosted a game under electric floodlights, in October 1878. Twelve lamps mounted on wooden gantries, two at each corner of the pitch and two behind each goal, were powered by batteries or steam engines. In his book

A History of Sheffield Football 1857–1889: Speed, Science and Bottom, Martin Westby says the illuminating power equalled '8,000 standard candles'. The local press enthused, 'Everybody seemed highly pleased with the result of the experiment, the light being most brilliant and effective. It may be stated that the experiment turned out to be a great financial success, the novelty of the thing drawing together an immense attendance, reaching in our estimation, nearly 20,000 people. When everything was in readiness, at 7.30 the distinguishing colours of the two sides were clearly visible, although it was rather difficult to discern the individual movement on the top side of the ground.' The Blues beat the Reds 2-0.

There were more experiments with floodlights over the next few years. At Blackburn they painted the ball white which helped a little but the technology was not reliable and many of these early games had to be abandoned. We may obsess with the sanctity of a Saturday three o'clock kick-off but, even then, clubs realised that they could increase revenue if games were played during weekday evenings – under artificial light of course. The Football League was having none of it and in its first season, 1888/89, it banned floodlights. Non-league clubs continued to experiment. In 1920 a women's game was played at Preston to raise money for unemployed ex-servicemen. To maximise gate receipts it was decided to make it a night game. The Secretary of State for War, Winston Churchill, gave permission for two anti-aircraft searchlights to be used to floodlight the game. For the record, Dick, Kerr Ladies beat a Rest of England team 4-0.

During the 1930s, Arsenal's pioneering manager Herbert Chapman had floodlights built into the West

Stand at Highbury. Southampton followed suit. They were deemed fine for training but the Football Association and the Football League continued to refuse permission for clubs to use them for official matches. It was not until well after the Second World War that they relented. The first league game under floodlights took place in 1956 between Portsmouth and Newcastle United. The early 'lights on poles' design were too low and caused problems with players being dazzled. This led to the building of the freestanding pylons which taper up to the lamps themselves. Now they too are being replaced by roof-mounted lights which are easier to maintain and direct.

I accept that floodlights are a strange interest to have but once you start noticing the shape and style of a stadium's illuminations it's difficult to stop. Groundhoppers share their latest finds not just from at home but from across the world and I have included a selection of them in the picture section of this book. There are some real gems to be found in eastern Europe where many teams have stuck with the freestanding pylon design. I admit that I visited Dynamo Berlin's stadium simply to see their floodlights. They sit in an inverted triangle, propped up on long, spindly tripods, seemingly defying gravity. Standing below them you feel they could come crashing down on you at any time. The lights in Hong Kong FC's Happy Valley ground are puny in comparison but they play beautifully against the backdrop of the high-rise flats beyond. Space is at a premium in the city-state so with no room for a base and a pylon they just build up.

The late Mark Watkins was a photographic chronicler of Cardiff City and published a book recording every detail of the old Ninian Park stadium before it was razed. His moody picture is taken from the club's main entrance on Sloper Road. To me it captures the promise of an evening kick-off, a little treat in the middle of the working week. The holiday postcard may have had its day. We now upload albums of ourselves to Facebook in real time. David Collins sent me a snap from La Linea de la Concepcion in southern Spain. It's a marvellous composition of palm trees and lights in the late afternoon. I have watched quite a bit of football in Serbia and games between Red Star and Partizan Belgrade are not for the fainthearted. Marko Mihaljevic's dusk over Partizan's Station JNA has caught the foreboding, bordering on fear which I get before the so-called 'Eternal Derby'.

Every stadium and every club, large or small, has a story to tell. You will probably have heard of Barnsley and their Oakwell home but perhaps not of BK Frem in Copenhagen or Aberdare Town. Fame or success in the traditional footballing sense, being in or near the top of the top league, is not the point here. The players and supporters of even the smallest team will have fond memories of their grounds. I got to spend an afternoon at each of these clubs and now too have a memory to share. The central picture in my collection takes me back many years when we 'broke' into the Hrazdan stadium in Yerevan, Armenia. The place had been so badly built that it could not be used for international football. It was the day after Wales had played at a much less imposing stadium on the other side of the city. Slightly hungover, we just walked into the Hrazdan only to be shooed out pretty sharpish by the groundsman, but not before we had got a picture of us kicking a ball below its massive lights.

So what is it about floodlights that excites us? Even if they are newly built, freestanding lights still hold a certain magic. They are interesting in themselves, in terms of scale and design, but I think their attraction is that they amplify the importance of a simple football match. Looking down from great heights these steel and glass behemoths guide and concentrate your focus on to the pitch. The game, any game, every game, is somehow magnified. They say 'this is a big deal' and that you are a part, however small a part, of it. Your tininess in comparison to the monumental setting around you may be part of the attraction – being a small part of a greater whole. I had a very uneasy feeling like that as I entered the Berlin Olympic Stadium, Albert Speer's Nazi architectural masterpiece, built for the 1936 Olympic Games and now home to Hertha Berlin.

Although there are no actual floodlights in it, I am drawn back to L.S. Lowry's painting *Going to the Match*. Completed in 1928, it shows fans walking to a traditional stadium, probably in Manchester. Young working-class men (for in the picture they are all men), fathers and sons, grandads too, are queuing up at turnstiles before squeezing into a steep open terrace. This is football idealised, as we imagine it back in its comparatively formative days. Even though by the 1920s it was already a professional game, teams were mostly made up of local players, clubs were an intrinsic part of society and attending a match was a communal experience. *Going to the Match* is owned by the Professional Footballers' Association but you can see it at The Lowry in Salford Quays.

Floodlights trigger a complex emotional response based on a real or imagined past. That it may include false memory doesn't matter. The imagery of the lost stadiums of Archibald Leitch carry us back to simpler times, when we stood shoulder to shoulder on packed terraces, when the only way to get the league results on Saturday evening was from the football 'pink' newspaper, as we sat in smoky pubs near the ground. What Leitch, the prodigious Scottish architect of many of our most famous stadiums, would have made of the homogenous modern footballing temples is anyone's guess. Is this all a case of invented memory? Am I rewriting our cultural history? Men with mufflers, kids using jumpers for goalposts, local lad made good by turning pro. Isn't it no more than nostalgia? Yes, probably. But every time I happen across an architectural football relic, floodlights and all, I get a warm, comforting feeling inside.

20

Bem-vindo Ao Brasil

THERE'S A theory in psychology called 'peak-end'. It goes like this: we judge and recall an experience based on our most intense memory of it, the *peak*, and/or the way it ends, the *end,* rather than on the whole event. For example, it doesn't matter how rubbish most of the holiday was, the moonlight party on the last night was superb. Or, the meal out was awful and the food was cold but we all remember where we were when John texted us that night to say he had just married Sue in Las Vegas. The peak experience then colours all the rest and, however grim the whole thing was, that's what you remember.

I think the peak-end theory explains how football's governing bodies, FIFA and UEFA down to the Premier League and the EFL, get away with treating fans as replaceable customers. The game is so ubiquitous and the numbers of supporters so large they know they can tell us to 'take it or leave it'. That's because at some point during a season or a tournament most of us will probably have an amazing experience. It could be your country beating a fierce rival; think England v Germany after a dismal campaign. For those of us with lower expectations, it would be Wales making it out of their qualifying group. On a club level there's that single, screaming goal in an otherwise unremarkable season.

Let me try to prove peak-end theory by taking you to a tournament in one of the most unequal footballing nations on Earth. *Bem-vindo ao Brasil* and the 2014 World Cup.

The promenade in Recife in the north-eastern province of Pernambuco was punctuated with little bars painted a dull blue. Small knots of people sat on stools drinking beer or coconut juice from cans looking across the golden sand. It was our first night in Brazil and a warm breeze welcomed Chester and I to the World Cup. The waves broke shallow on the long beach. A young couple danced the samba back and forth across the narrow prom. They barely looked up as they spidered in, out and around each other.

World Cup fever was everywhere. Giant banners and yellow and green bunting were strung between the lampposts, and flapped around kiosks and shops. The Brazilian flag has a blue globe in the middle with 27 stars across it. They represent the constellations in the southern hemisphere as seen from Rio de Janeiro in the early hours of 15 November 1889, the day the country became a republic. The country's slogan, 'Ordem e Progresso', translated as 'Order and Progress', is written across the sphere. Flags blew on street corners and from the windows of the high-rise flats. I had a feeling that if Brazil did not win the World Cup there would be a lot of disappointed people.

On the beach, a gang of children were playing football between two sets of twisted sticks banged into the sand.

There were no touchlines marked out and every so often the ball went into the sea. The kids didn't care and ran in to retrieve it, their shirts billowing in the wind before they hit the spray. Back on the beach, one lad went through down the right but, rather than place the ball at his mate's left foot which would have guaranteed a goal, he stopped it dead in the sand. He paused and then chipped it over the goalkeeper's head. It seems this nation's silky skills are indeed honed on the beach. These lads were about 13 or 14 years old. It was ten o'clock at night. Was there no school tomorrow? Maybe they had a week off for the start of the World Cup.

We had been warned by family, friends and the football fraternity to be careful in Brazil. Even the tourist office at the airport told us we would not be safe walking to our hotel. This was not just the usual petty crime and pickpocket stuff. The whole country was supposedly in revolt. Anti-FIFA, anti-government, anti-slum clearance. I was confused. It was early on but from what we had seen so far, Brazil was actually rather calm. It certainly didn't feel dangerous.

We walked back to the hotel and I picked up a newspaper in reception. It told a different story. The front page showed the fourth day of a metro strike in São Paulo. Trade unionists were waving a red flag as tear gas rained down. With the main transport system out of action, the people had taken to the streets, some to protest, but mostly to use the bus network to get to work. The result was gridlock and chaos. The number of these demonstrations may have been slowing down as the World Cup approached but this was not the face of a stable and dynamic country that Brazil or FIFA wanted to show us.

The next day we walked along the same beach where we had seen the dancers. In daylight, the prom was like a retirement village. Older men and women strolled between the cafes. One man stopped to talk to us. 'You're okay on this part of the beach,' he said. 'But don't go down there.' He pointed south to where the high-rises stopped, to be replaced by low-level, scruffy buildings with corrugated roofs. 'There's a favela down there and last week I saw an old woman held up at gunpoint. In broad daylight. They just drove off on a motorbike. There's one up there too,' he said, pointing in the opposite direction. We got the message, left the beach and went into town.

On the bus, we started chatting to Daniel Cabral, a young photographer who had good English and was keen to talk. 'What do people make of the World Cup?' Chester asked him. 'Do you think it's all a waste of money?'

'Our public services and schools are in a really poor state,' Daniel said. 'And then they go and spend all that money on a football tournament. It's not just in Rio or São Paolo, you know. There've been protests here in Recife too. Yes. Riots, tear gas and all that. Terrible. If you'd asked me what I thought about it all a week ago I'd have given you a different answer. Now though, we're all right behind the national team.'

For months the media had been questioning Brazil's ability to stage the World Cup. Many of the trumpeted infrastructure projects, roads, railways and the smartening up of cities, which were part of the original bid, had been abandoned. These were supposed to be the lasting legacy of World Cup 2014. The footballing cartel who run the game in Brazil are called the 'top hats' in Portuguese and were said to be in hock with the politicians. All of them, in one way or another, were making a fortune on the back of the tournament while the bulk of the population got poorer. Trickle-down economics? I don't think so. Most people we met seemed resigned to it all. There's an expression in Brazil, 'Ele rouba mas faz', which roughly translates as 'He steals but he gets things done'.

If only they did get things done. Our first match was in Natal, a three-and-a-half-hour drive north of Recife. We stayed on the sweeping bay of Porta Negra. Mexico were playing Cameroon and the party was in full swing when we arrived. A mariachi band strummed and hooted furiously, beer bottles clanked and lads and lasses from all corners of the globe held their own qualifier, kicking a ball on the beach. 'Have you got a ticket?' I asked one guy who was staying in our hotel. 'No, but I'll take my chance on the gate,' he said.

An American from Boston was in full flow at the bar. 'Soccer is not having a renaissance in America,' he said defiantly. 'It never went away.' Most of the Mexicans I met were actually Americans. I did not meet anyone from Cameroon at the pre-match party.

It bucketed down with rain the day of the game. The approaches to the Estadio das Dunas had not been finished. The kerbstones lay higgledy piggledy at the side of the road allowing the rain to turn the uneven pavements into small rivers. We stepped up, down and around the road to try to keep our feet and then our legs dry. Sands, bricks and razor wire had been left in piles where the contractors had dropped them off. Would they ever get the job finished? Did it really matter?

Rows of bored police stood under trees and bus stops, taking what shelter they could. Their machine guns were at the ready, a helicopter buzzed overhead, and there was even a gunboat in the bay. None of this of course would be shown on TV. Nothing was going to spoil this worldwide advertisement for Brazil. On the pitch and despite having two goals disallowed, Mexico beat Cameroon by a single strike from Oribe Peralta. It was not the unfinished streets or getting soaked as they queued for more than an hour that all those Mexican Americans would remember. No, it would be the event, the victory and the celebration. That's all that mattered.

It was the same a few days later at the Pernambuco stadium back in Recife. Japan v Côte d'Ivoire. To get to the match you had to first buy a train ticket and be fitted with a red wristband. The metro stopped at several stations for minutes on end and when the train finally drew to a halt you had to catch a bus to the stadium itself. Well, actually not to the stadium itself. You were teased by the sparkling lights in the distance, tantalisingly close but still a good 20-minute walk away. Cue more queuing. There were police and barriers and stewards pushing you around but no one really knew what was going on.

Inside, we left our cheap seats in the upper stand behind the goal and strolled down to the side of the pitch to dance with the Ivorians. I'd have been damned annoyed if I had paid top dollar for my ticket only for the likes of me to amble up alongside them in the posh seats. It finished 2-1 to Côte d'Ivoire and though, few in numbers, both sets of supporters were superb. The unselfconscious enthusiasm of the Japanese took me back to their own World Cup in

2002. It is as if they have just discovered the game and are making up for the years of football they have lost out on. It's an almost innocent, childlike passion. The Ivorians played their part too, dancing, drumming and blasting on a massive horn all through the game. We swung and shouted with them and if they were annoyed that we had gatecrashed their party, they didn't show it.

Next stop for us was the colonial city of Salvador. Five hundred years ago Portuguese invaders brought slaves from the port here up to the main square to be sold to plantation owners. Tonight it was a different kind of invasion. There were just 24 hours before Portugal played Germany and the beer and caipirinhas were flowing. As far as chants go, 'Deutschland, Deutschland' is pretty basic, but for a country which for decades denied itself any public demonstration of national pride it was good to see the amber, black and red flag being waved with gusto.

There was a campaign some years ago to stop inter-club rivalry at Wales national games. The 'Wear Red for Wales' campaign urged supporters not to don the white kits of Swansea or the blue of Cardiff at internationals. It worked, though I hate the term 'Red Wall' the marketers now use for the Wales fans. The Germans needed no such directive. If the guys wearing Schalke, Rot-Weiss and Duisburg shirts who we drank with wanted to kick six bells out of each other, it wasn't going to happen at the World Cup. There was only one team in town tonight.

Salvador was a refreshing change on our tour of Brazil. The ground was just a few hundred metres from the historic centre and on matchday, beer in hand, we ambled our way through the cobbled streets to the Itaipava Arena

Fonte Nova stadium. Along the way music pumped up the atmosphere from bars and the windows of private homes. The old buildings looked down on the booming party as we danced and whooped in the square. It felt like the whole city had come out to join us. I wondered if the locals were supporting Portugal as their 'mother' country but it looked like the party itself was more important than any football result.

A young woman with her back to us cradled a small child in her arms. When she turned round I was amazed to see that the boy's eyes were a radiant, emerald green. The colour is thought to have come down the male line of the descendants of Dutch settlers in Brazil. The very presence of a green-eyed boy is supposed to bring you good luck. So the gods were on our side! After the initial shock we smiled and I think I followed everyone else's lead and stroked the lad's hair. It was great to be mingling and sharing a beer with the local people in a genuinely welcoming city.

Everyone was on a high that day in Salvador and it was to provide a peak footballing memory too, as Germany's Thomas Müller scored a hat-trick to destroy ten-man Portugal. We came out of the stadium buzzing and not just because of the white rum and beer we had drunk. This was the World Cup we had crossed the Atlantic to find. That day still sticks in my mind as one of *the* football experiences.

The national stadium in Brasilia, too, was within walking distance of the centre, if indeed that futuristic capital can be said to have a centre. But there, as in Belo Horizonte, we were pushed around and forced to queue for hours in the blazing sun to get in. Do we football fans surrender our human rights the moment we buy a match ticket? I can't imagine someone going to the opera and being treated like this. There was a lone protester outside the stadium in Belo. He sat on his bike holding a homemade placard. His silent protest read 'Fuck FIFA'. We bought a beer from the street seller next to him, chuckled and walked on.

By chance, in Manaus, we met up with some fellow Welsh fans, exchanged travel stories and, of course, regretted our own nation's absence from the big stage. The city had set up two big screens in the square outside the famous opera house. Chairs had been laid out for us to watch one of two matches being shown. All was well until the party came to an abrupt halt. At about 11 o'clock all the bars closed as police cars circled the square sounding their sirens. The deafening tactic worked, the square was cleared and we wound our way home.

There had been civil disorder in Brazil for months and I suppose they thought that late nights, alcohol and football offered a high-profile stage for further protests. But the authorities' response (and it would be the same four years later at the World Cup in Russia) in the town centres and in the grounds was way over the top. Outside each stadium there were rows of traffic police, the Policia Rodoviaria in well-pressed khaki trousers. Behind them stood small groups of Policia Militar who wore blue helmets and had batons at the ready. Another meaner-looking crowd wore red berets tight over their shaved heads. If this presence was meant to be intimidating it was working. Long after the game in Belo, a group of us sat at an open-air burger bar in a smart residential area. A 4x4 police car drove up and parked alongside us. A young policeman in full uniform and armed to the teeth came out and stood alongside us, leaning on the car. He was relaxed and smiled. We had been given our own security detail.

The whole country appeared resigned to this constant state of siege. Brazil was under military dictatorship from 1964–1982. The upside of authoritarian rule and the restriction of freedoms was the 'Brazilian Miracle', 20 years of economic development compressed into just five. More recently the country has been lauded as one of the so-called BRICS countries (Brazil, Russia, India, China and South Africa), the world's five emerging economic powerhouses. But there's a cost involved in the race for growth – inequality, jealousy and crime. Guns beget guns and even the poorer houses, perhaps because they were poor, had their windows barred and were topped with razor wire.

Before I went to Brazil I read Jorge Amado's *The Violent Land* which describes the murderous competition between two families for control of the cocoa plantations in the early years of the 20th century. He says the southern part of the state of Bahia was 'fertilised with blood', that the whole country was built on a brutal past and that this common history has been accepted unquestioned. Has violence become normalised in the decades since then? Were the Brazilian people accepting their own environmental destruction, huge disparities in income and corruption as a price worth paying for continuing growth? The excesses of the 2014 World Cup could be seen as a small price and one worth paying for a month in the international limelight.

I have written about how Gabon built ridiculous stadiums which would hardly be used after they had hosted the Africa Cup of Nations. There was talk of corruption in high places and that ticket prices were beyond the reach of locals but the accepted narrative was that 'All went well. Football was the winner.'

Devon Rowcliffe has written about the continuing cost to South Korea of co-hosting the World Cup in 2002 with Japan. Stadiums with 50,000 seats were built in cities across the country. These showcase arenas, with a running track and moat between the stands and the pitch, were wholly inappropriate for football. To justify the expenditure, teams in the K League have been forced to relocate from their traditional grounds to the new creations. For years crowds of just a few thousand rattled around the empty spaces. Eventually clubs moved back to smaller venues. The result – a string of fine, expensive stadiums which are barely used. The same of course would be true in Brazil. How did they, how do they, still get away with it?

Now if you take in isolation the best experiences we had in Brazil – those few days in Salvador, marching with the mariachi band in Porta Negra and the chance meetings with Welsh supporters in Manaus – then the World Cup was a massive success. Take the worst of it – the scramble for tickets, queuing for hours in the rain, rip-off hotel prices and being pushed this way and that – then it was a disaster. Not forgetting all the time we spent, as we had been advised to, looking over our shoulders. Remember the drug-related crime, riots and terrorists? The whole thing was expensive, relentless and at times unnerving. But unless you were actually there you would never have known any of this.

I also wonder if our experiences are distorted by what it all looks like on TV, even if we were at the game and saw something quite different. Television had taught me very early on in life that football in Brazil was beautiful. Think

Pelé, Jairzinho and anything to do with the 1970 World Cup. At the very end of a tournament you won't remember the hours of desperate 0-0 draws you watched. No, it will be the best bits crushed into a finely crafted minute-and-a-half musical montage, ending of course with the cup being raised in triumph. Peak. End.

In the corridors of corporate power and on the private aircraft chartered to and from matches, this World Cup, like all the others, was seen as another stunning success. I too have ironed my memories to smooth out the unpleasant parts, only remembering the peak experiences. Never mind the cost to the Brazilian government or the bill its citizens would eventually have to pick up, in FIFA's eyes the tournament paid for itself and television audiences were as high as ever. But I have a nagging feeling that in going to Brazil I had been complicit in mortgaging a nation's future for the sake of a month-long sporting jamboree. FIFA wanted it, the Brazilian government wanted it, I had wanted it and, at least while the whole thing lasted, the people had wanted it. I loved the World Cup but I still can't help feeling guilty somehow.

21

Foxes And Bluebirds

ON 27 October 2018 a helicopter took off from the King Power Stadium in Leicester. The city's football team had just played West Ham United and the club's billionaire Thai owner, Vichai Srivaddhanaprabha, was going home. He often travelled to and from matches this way and, according to the *Leicester Mercury*, the helicopter was 'a familiar sight for Foxes fans'. Accompanying Srivaddhanaprabha were two members of his staff, the pilot and another passenger. Within seconds of taking off, the helicopter spiralled out of control and crashed in a fireball. Everyone on board died. As a mark of respect Leicester's next fixture against Southampton was cancelled. There was then a debate as to whether they should play Cardiff City just a week after the tragedy. I for one was glad they did and I wrote this tribute after a sad but strangely uplifting afternoon:

'Look! They've all worn the away strip for today,' said the old man behind me. I looked across to my left to the Leicester supporters in the away section and they were indeed all wearing the same colour shirts. But it was not the team's regular grey away strip, rather white T-shirts bearing a picture of their late chairman Vichai Srivaddhanaprabha. There was also a tribute to him written across every chest in a simple two-word message, 'The Boss'.

It was always going to be an awkward match. Over a pre-match pint of Gower Gold Ale we wondered how both teams might react, how we as fans would react. Cardiff needed three points from this game in their fight against relegation from the Premier League. I think the Leicester players just needed to get out there and play. I needn't have worried about the reaction. The Cardiff City supporters, so often considered the bad boys of football, got their response to the tragedy just right.

As the teams ran out, a huge flag, 30 metres wide and eight metres long, was rolled back from the front seats over the heads of us Cardiff fans in the middle section of the Ninian Stand. It was a massive Thai national flag, either side of which were the crests of the home and away clubs and the words 'RIP Vichai'. The low autumn sun was blocked out for a moment as I lifted my hands and helped to roll the giant banner back. It was a moving experience, as if touching the flag added some physical contact to the shared emotions buzzing around us. The man in front of me dabbed a tear from his eye.

The banner was moved sideways and crossed into the away end. The Leicester fans had unfurled their own flag with a club logo on it and in the same way as we had, they passed it over their heads into our section. Two teams, two sets of fans, two rivals were exchanging battle colours as we came together to share the grief of a whole city. Wreaths were laid in the centre circle, the minute's silence was immaculately observed, the referee's whistle blew and then it was down to business. In the week since Srivaddhanaprabha's death some commentators said that the game itself was unimportant, but that wasn't true. The players certainly didn't think so. In the greater scheme of things of course this match was an irrelevance, but it was also a form of release and both teams gave it their all.

Perhaps under the circumstances it was right that Leicester won. When Demarai Gray scored in the 55th minute he pulled up his jersey to reveal an undershirt bearing the words 'For Khun Vichai'. The Leicester fans continued to sing his name for the rest of the highly charged and poignant afternoon. Many of them stayed behind at the final whistle and applauded the Leicester players and staff as their thoughts turned to Vichai's funeral in Thailand.

It can be trite, a cliché even, to talk about people 'coming together through sport'. But not for the first time, this match made me feel part of an extended football family. The game has had its fair share of tragedies down the years. The Munich air crash of 1958 and the death of the Busby Babes is part of Manchester United's rich and sometimes tragic history. As a child I remember the flickering black and white pictures of the Ibrox Stadium disaster in Glasgow in 1971 when 66 people died. The Bradford City fire in 1985 killed 56 spectators and injured a further 265. Just a week before that Leicester game I had been at Anfield for Cardiff's game at the famous stadium. Outside the ground I saw young men and women who weren't even born in 1989 make the sign of the cross before the memorial to the Hillsborough disaster when 96 Liverpool supporters went to watch a football match but never came home. All these events have become shared national memories and the grieving of the families and friends directly involved too has been shared.

Whatever our differences and club rivalries, as fans we understand football's relevance beyond the field of play. It may be the ubiquity of the game, its international profile, families watching six-year-olds at mini-football, but somehow and especially at times of tragedy, the game has the power to bring strangers together to share a common grief, to share our common humanity.

22

The Streets Of Sarajevo

IN 2013 I joined a group of supporters on a drive to Skopje where Wales were to play Macedonia. Ours was one half of a two-car convoy from Gôl Cymru, the fans' charity, which was again crossing Europe visiting children's homes en route with gifts and donations. On these journeys we always try to watch a match somewhere along the way. Plotting a path which takes in a game is not always that easy. The dates don't fit or the game you want to see is due to be played just after you will have left the city. So we were feeling rather smug when we had the chance to take in a match at Sarajevo, and it was a derby at that. What I didn't know at the time was how closely linked FK Sarajevo was to my own Cardiff City FC.

The approach to the Otoka football ground took us past the mighty Istiklal džamija mosque. A gift from the Indonesian people, its two towering minarets guard a wide, black, central dome. As the football fans in their red and white scarves straggled past the mosque, a wedding party spilled out through its heavy double doors. The young men were dressed in dark suits, some women wore a full niqab, others simple headscarves. One woman stood out. She was wearing a very short, yellow miniskirt and tottered on her high heels as she came down the steps. The image seemed to be making an unintended statement, 'There is no one kind of Muslim in Sarajevo. You want to cover your face? Okay. You want to show off your legs? That's okay too.' And as we waited for kick-off in the away stand, the Muslim call to afternoon prayer reverberated from the minarets across the pitch towards us.

This Saturday, the capital's third team, Olimpik Sarajevo, were hosting local rivals and the runners-up of last year's Bosnian Premier League, FK Sarajevo. Both clubs were formed out of war, Olimpik in October 1993 during the siege of Sarajevo, while FK was set up in the nascent Yugoslavia just after the Second World War. Now football in these parts is intertwined with history. During the Bosnian war both sides recruited street fighters from football clubs. The groups of supporters called themselves 'ultras', the European shorthand for passionate fans, mostly loud and peaceful but sometimes violent too. FK Sarajevo's 'Hordes of Evil' joined the Bosnian government side, as did the 'Maniacs' of Zeljeznicar, FK's main rivals. But that was then wasn't it? History, as they say.

Two flares fizzed in the middle of the packed terrace spewing pink smoke over the crowd and across the pitch, obscuring the green playing surface. As one, the supporters started a low, guttural chant, and then they stopped. There was a second of cold silence before a single sharp drumbeat. The crack of the drum like a single rifle shot echoed back from the opposite terrace heralding another

I'll say it again. Wales v Spain, 11 October 2018.

First clear the goats. Football Gambian style. Serrekunda East Park Stadium, 9 February 2019.

At last. Completing the 92. The Hive Stadium, home of Barnet FC

Homeless World Cup Cardiff, July 2019

With actor and activist Michael Sheen at the Homeless World Cup.

This game changes lives. Offering hope at the Homeless World Cup.

India national homeless team. Cardiff 2019.

Floodlight Porn.

Groundhopping in the shadow of the steelworks, East Cardiff. Bridgend Street FC 2 v Goytre 2 in the Welsh League. 1 February 2020.

A riot of colour. World Cup Brazil 2020.

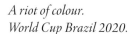

Germany 4 v Portugal 0. Arena Fonte Nova, Salvador, Brazil. World Cup, 16 June 2014.

Not everyone's happy. Belo Horizonte, World Cup Brazil 2014.

The Germans travel in numbers.

Wales supporters' charity Gôl Cymru at the Central Model School, Dublin. October 2018

Gôl Cymru visiting Ahmet and friends. Belgrade, Serbia.

*Red Star v
FK Partizan.
Marakana
Stadium, Belgrade,
12 September
2015.*

*The Eternal derby.
FK Partizan v Red
Star Belgrade.*

A sight I thought I would never see. Wales at a major finals. Euro 2016.

Time to celebrate. Wales 3 v Russia 0. Stadium de Toulouse, 20 June 2016.

The 'Red Wall' at Euro 2016.

We're Cardiff City. We'll always be blue.

If only we could bottle the joy of following Wales.

Wales fans on their way to the Cardiff City Stadium.

round of chanting. The fans were egged on by a man with a megaphone precariously hanging from a post at pitchside. The almost military precision of the performance was just a little unsettling.

We stood among the FK faithful who filled the larger side of this tiny stadium. Olimpik have very few fans and, despite this being a home game, on today's evidence even fewer who would openly show their allegiance. 'Imagine this at home,' said one of our group, Kevin Davies, a fellow Cardiff City supporter. 'Going to a game in your own stadium and not being able to shout for your team. Not much point going is there?' Everyone around us was certainly wearing the maroon shirts of FK rather than the home team's kit. Like most groundhoppers Kevin is a treasure trove of obscure and, probably because of that, fascinating facts about the game. Apparently, as FK was a latecomer to the footballing scene in Bosnia, having only been founded in 1946, maroon was chosen for their playing strip because every other colour kit was already 'taken' by the league's clubs. FK won their first championship in what was Yugoslavia in 1967. There was a bit of a wait for their second national honours when they again topped the Yugoslav First League in 1985.

More interesting to me was the fact that the year we visited, 2013, FK Sarajevo were bought by the Malaysian billionaire Tan Sri Vincent Tan, the major shareholder of our very own Cardiff City. He immediately dissolved Sarajevo's long-standing steering committee and supervisory board and appointed Ken Choo, Cardiff's chief executive officer, as one of the club's five new directors. His money, his club. As Tan had told me during his wholly unnecessary and divisive rebranding of the Bluebirds, 'I control this club. If you don't like it then find another owner.'

Under the takeover of Sarajevo, Tan would continue the club's community work, invest in the team and there would be exchanges of players between both teams. In fact, there was a match between the two clubs the very next year. Wearing shirts sporting the logo of the sponsor of both teams, Visit Malaysia, FK played a friendly against Cardiff's under-21s and beat them 4-1.

Tan's control of Sarajevo proved successful. They won the Bosnia and Herzegovina Cup in 2014 and the Premier League in 2015. Images of Tan being carried shoulder-high through the streets of Sarajevo wrapped in a swirling maroon fog from the fans' flares made it into the media back home. It was the kind of adoration I think he was looking for when he had entered football. Cardiff City FC of course duly sent its official congratulations. The response from the rest of us was a little more muted. Since March 2019, FK Sarajevo have been owned by the Vietnamese businessman Nguyễn Hoài Nam. Another club, another business, another owner. Such is the way of football even in the more lowly European leagues.

The game we watched was not much to write home about but, despite the poor performances, there was a fiery passion in the crowd. Every decision the referee made was contested. Firecrackers punctuated the singing and the game had to be stopped more than once as flares were thrown on to the pitch. A dumpy fireman would waddle on with a bucket of sand and giant tongs, lift the flare into the bucket and carry it to safety. It seemed just as routine as the trainer coming on, spraying a player's ankle and then jogging off.

Back home having a game stopped because of pyrotechnics would have been national news and those responsible facing prison terms and lengthy football banning orders. But this was Sarajevo and the players just used the stop in play to draw breath and have a sip of water.

FK won 2-0 in what was a pretty nothingy game. Despite the win the referee and linesmen were pelted with bottles, coins and goodness knows what else as they made their way off the pitch. Police and officials had to shield them as they ran to the safety of the plastic-covered tunnel. There was a venom in the crowd but, with no home supporters to be seen, there was no one really to direct it at. It was as if these young men were acting out their own part in a strange, stylised performance: a theatre of hate without a victim, just the pantomime villain that was the poor referee. In his dystopian novel *1984*, George Orwell wrote about the 'Two Minutes Hate'. Every morning, party members gathered together to vent their hatred of an imaginary enemy shouting abuse at a single figure on a huge screen. It was a daily outlet for the people's anger and frustration. Has football in Sarajevo become the weekly Ninety Minutes Hate?

Richard Mills from the University of East Anglia has published an academic paper called 'Fighters, footballers and nation builders: wartime football in the Serb-held territories of the former Yugoslavia, 1991–1996'. He says that the outbreak of war in Yugoslavia had a devastating effect on all forms of cultural life, including football. Yet, in spite of the raging conflict, the game continued to be an important aspect of everyday life throughout the region.

Mills argues that in the newly emerging Republika Srpska and Republika Srpska Krajina, the Serb-held territories of

Bosnia and Herzegovina and Croatia, football was a morale-booster providing soldiers with a distraction from fighting on the front. But it also served a higher cause. Via league and cup competitions, football assisted in the creation of ethnically homogeneous regions. Alongside media coverage of the games themselves the competitions helped map the 'imagined communities'. Mills says that during those war years football was being used as symbolic proof that all Serbs continued to belong to Yugoslavia. He writes, 'The game, and the sporting press that wrote about it, also provided an ideal subject for propaganda about enemy nations and a platform from which journalists could expound the necessities of the unification of all Serb states.'

The young men, and some women, with whom we stood on the terrace of the Otoka football ground, were Sarajevo's 'lads', the hardcore, who just a few years ago would have been firing or cowering from real munitions. Perhaps these games provide an outlet, a release of emotion for all the hatred which had so recently led to murder, rape and genocide. Is football a metaphor for war? I don't know, but better this bit of play-acting than the real thing.

23

The Football Family

THERE'S NO single kind of football supporter. And thank
God for that. From non-league devotees to those who spend
a fortune following their team in the Premier League, nerdy
groundhoppers and fans who only follow their national team
when they are winning, it takes all sorts. With my tongue
firmly in cheek I decided to take a closer look at some of my
fellow football travellers. Do you recognise yourself?

Ethan
'Hi. My name's Ethan. I'm 28 and I've been supporting
Liverpool for about five years. I used to support Chelsea but
then Mourinho went and left and it all went to pot down
"the Bridge". See I want to support a winner. Like life really.
You don't want to be associated with losers do you? I played
a bit of football at school. I was never any good but I love
watching the game on TV. I've got Sky, BT, the lot. Well
you've got to these days to be able to watch it all. My mates
take the mickey out of me when Liverpool lose but I don't
care because we're the champions.

'I live in a nice semi on the edge of town. I've got a lovely looking wife, Kayleigh, and we've just taken delivery of a new baby boy. We bought him the full red baby kit at Christmas and put his name on the back. He looks so cute! My car's a second-hand BMW and of course it's covered in Liverpool stickers. I'm proud to support my team. Mind you, I only wear the team colours when we play or when I go on holiday to Dubai. During the season, if the match is on a Monday or Tuesday night I'll go to the pub to watch it. There's a crowd of us Liverpool supporters in there and The Lion is rammed. You should see the place when Salah smashes one in. Mayhem.

'What I love about the game is winning. That's what's great about the Premier League and the Champions League isn't it? It's for the winners, the big boys. I love watching it on the telly. It's all there for you, the replays, slow-motion, stats, close-ups of the players. And it's on almost every night. The best teams in the world. That Covid thing could have been a downer what with the stadiums being empty but it didn't matter that much to me. My routine didn't change from the regular season really. Grab a can, Kayls makes me a sandwich, put my feet up and switch on. Don't tell anyone but I had a couple of the lads over during lockdown to watch the Reds. Me, I didn't believe any of that government scaremongering stuff anyhow.

'I work in IT in the Sony factory and, say this quietly, I'm looking for promotion really soon. Some of the boys in work support the Saddlers [Walsall]. Saddos more like. We all talk about the games during breaks at work. Of course they know all about Liverpool 'cos we're on the telly all the time. Some of the lads play a bit and another guy referees on Saturday mornings. It's not for me though. I prefer golf. In fact I'm doing nine holes with the boss this weekend. Fingers crossed, if you know what I mean.

'Have I been to Anfield? Erm. Can't get tickets just like that can you. And what with the baby and all, it's a bit far just for a game if truth be told. I mean, to Liverpool from here in Walsall like.'

Mandy

'I'm Mandy. I'm 31 and I've been playing football for about seven years now. I loved the game as a kid. My family was nuts about it, Dad and two brothers too, but it wasn't a thing for girls to play back then was it? After I left school I started training with a couple of the lasses from work. Did I say? I'm a teacher in a secondary school. Yeah, you guessed it. PE. After a few months of five-a-side we formed a proper team and now we're playing twice a week. It's not a league as such. More like a series of friendlies. My partner Pete complains I put too much into the game, but I say "you only live once".

'They're a great bunch, the girls. We go to the pub after training, just one or two mind because we're all driving. The only pitch we can get is miles away. The ones nearby have all been booked by the lads years since. We talk about football all the time. Girly things too, but it's the football that brings us together.

'I'm really interested in the technical aspects of the game – formations, turning defence into attack, how to motivate players, that kind of thing. I can use it all in school too. I'm really lucky that my interest and work kind of go together. I'll watch football on the box. In fact I watch it most nights, especially when Pete's tired. I prefer games from the Championship and lower leagues. All that Premier stuff is a bit too inch-perfect for me. It's like a video game. The teams a bit lower down the footballing ladder make more mistakes. It sounds odd but I can somehow relate to that. It's also the range of teams you get in the lower leagues, and players you may recognise, but haven't seen in a while. Some are on their way up, others on their way down. Pete says I should stop watching so much of it on the telly and get a proper hobby.

'I've got a lovely Fiat 500. White. I give two of the girls, Sharon and Anna, a lift to matches. We're all pretty much the same really, getting on with life and work. The kids' stuff can wait a while, though Pete keeps saying "the clock's ticking, love" which really annoys me.

'I'm not sure me and the girls are mad-keen supporters of any particular team. If you pushed me I suppose I'd go for Gillingham. They've got that gorgeous centre-half but of course you're not supposed to say that kind of thing these days. No, it's the game itself rather than any team that we're all into.

'Pete likes the football but he smashed his ankle two years ago and had to give it up. He's supportive of me, sort of, but I think it hurts him to see me coming home shattered after training, and him like, you know, not being able to play. It's not resentment really but I can tell he doesn't like it. We'll work it all out though. I know we will.'

Jack

'I suppose you'd call me a football bore because I really, no I mean *really*, love the game. Everything about it. My name's Jack, named after Jackie Charlton, my grampa's favourite player. I kid you not. I'll watch any kind of football, kids on the parks, non-league, QPR of course, *Match of the Day*, the lot. But my favourite really is the European game. I follow clubs and players across the continent. It doesn't have to be the top-end stuff. Oh no, I'm just as interested in the little fish, more so than your Juves and Barças.

'I've watched so much of it over the years I think I understand the dynamics of the leagues in different countries. You've got the top teams in Spain, then England, Germany and Italy of course, but within those countries there's another layer of the game and it's great to see the little clubs emerging. It can take years but every now and again you spot a team in the qualifiers or group stages of the Europa League and you say, "Yep, they're gonna make it if that manager stays with them and they get a decent striker." It's like a game of chess, football, isn't it?

'I'm 45 now and work in menswear in a department store. Assistant manager. Not sure I'll make much more than that, to be honest, but it's a living isn't it? Working in menswear I get a staff discount so I'm usually in a plain pair of trousers with a nice shirt and tie. Suits are a bit stuffy aren't they? "Sensible" shoes of course, what with all that standing around. There's no one really to talk to in work and I don't go out that much so I suppose football is my real friend. Debbie in accounts said the game was my surrogate girlfriend. Honestly!

'At home I collect football tickets and programmes. I sell quite a few on eBay. It's a hobby but I can make a bit of extra cash on the side too. When I've saved up enough I treat myself to a football weekend abroad. They call us "ground-hoppers". I've seen teams that most people don't know exist play, teams like Poggibonsi in Italy and Gloria Buzău in Romania. I actually saw the Lebanon FA Cup semi-final in the Beirut Municipal Stadium. What a place that was. We've got a groundhopper app for it all and we post pictures and stories of where we've been, on social media. The last game I saw was Oldenburg against Teutonia Otten in Germany's northern regional division. The game was nothing to write home about but it was a lovely stadium.

'My wife Moira left me three years ago and I'm not that interested in starting over in that department to be honest with you. She joked at the time that my replica shirt collection came between us. Did I tell you I have more than 50 of them? English, European and a few from South America. I got the Boca Juniors shirt online but my favourite's got to be the one signed by the whole QPR promotion team of 2011. That particular beauty of course has been framed. I think Moira was trying to be ironic about the shirts thing. Or maybe she was trying to break the news to me gently. It still hurt though. Ah well, only six more weeks until the Belgrade derby.'

24

Merci Cymru

FOR SOME it is a long holiday in the sun with their young family. For others their wedding day and honeymoon – perfect experiences where something utterly personal but defining happens and they stay with you for life. The further away you get from them, the deeper your remembered emotions run. Love, warmth, happiness; the memories grow rosier by the year. I of course have had a few of these 'perfect moments' as the actor Spalding Gray calls them. He says you must savour them as they only happen once or twice in a whole lifetime. I had a lovely wedding day in glorious sunshine, and Chester's birth, though not without its problems, was a joyous occasion. However, the standout time of my life was the summer of 2016, and yes, it was all to do with football.

I didn't understand how much Wales's French adventure was to affect me until some months after the event. I edited a book of supporters' memories of the European Championship called *Merci Cymru* but I had difficulty setting down what it all meant to me. Those three weeks brought together my family, friends and my national team. At the time it all felt too intimate to communicate, too difficult to get right but there was one experience which might help explain what that summer meant to me.

It was a warm Thursday afternoon in August 2016 and I was walking in a field outside the border town of Abergavenny when it happened. For those of you who know what the Eisteddfod Maes is, it needs little explanation. But for those who don't, here goes. Forget the flowing robes and bardic bullshit, the real attraction of Wales's annual cultural festival is walking around the Maes, a field dotted with rows of stalls, music stages and bars. It is home to Welsh culture for a whole week. The joy of the Eisteddfod is in just talking to friends from years ago and bumping into others who may be just acquaintances. Avoiding the ones you don't want to see as you drag yourself around the tents for the umpteenth time, mind, is an art in itself.

The sun shone, choral music drifted across the well-worn field and that's when it happened. Ifor Roberts, from Machynlleth, was deep in conversation with another guy outside a tent selling t-shirts. I remember this because the stand was run by a company called Shwldimwl. Its owner, Owain Young, regularly updates his stock with inventive and cheeky Wales football designs. There's a bearded Joe Allen, Gareth Bale celebrating a free kick and a series with 'I am Welsh not English' written in the language of whichever team Wales are about to play.

I had only ever met Ifor Roberts once before – on a busy street in the city of Lyon in the south of France barely a month earlier. In the glorious evening sunshine on the banks of the Rhone we'd discussed Wales's chances against

Portugal that night, his stomping ground of mid-Wales and the worst hotel I had ever stayed in not far from his home, in Corris.

On that dusty field on the Welsh borders we caught each other's eye and without a word passing between us he winked at me and I nodded at him. No words. Just a recognition. Because we had something in common. We had both been there, had been part of the journey. We had both seen the Wales national team not only qualify for, but go on to reach, the semi-finals of the European Championships. And if you have followed Welsh football for as long as Ifor and I had, then that was something very special. We didn't need to speak. We would be pals forever. I walked on feeling good about the world.

I spoke to more than one supporter that week who'd had similar experiences. There was a private code between us, a nod of recognition to remember that glorious summer of football. Summer of Love? Well, add to that, Wales's Summer of Success 2016. The team's performance and the devotion shown by the fans are now part of our collective history. People from all over Wales had been part of it. In the open-air fanzone in Cardiff, in pubs and clubs and at home, men, women and children came together for a party which seemed like it would never end. 'Wasn't it just – brilliant?' my good friend Hannah said when we finally came home from France. She'd watched every game on TV with her two little girls Manon and Gwenno, kitted out in their Wales tops. And she doesn't even like football.

In the beginning there was Bordeaux, where we played our first match of the finals against Slovakia. That's not strictly true. Wales's road to France 2016 really started in

Zenica, in Bosnia-Herzegovina, nine months earlier. Six hundred of we faithful crammed into a corner of the Bilino Polje stadium in the pouring rain. We actually lost our last qualifying match 2-0 but it didn't matter because other results went our way and we were on our way to France. For many of us though, the journey started even before that, in bizarre places like Belarus and Armenia, on cold nights watching Wales lose yet again in Cardiff, getting beaten 4-0 by Italy in Bologna (and then again by the same margin in Milan) and in so many other forsaken places across Europe. Through the fallow years of Welsh football in the 1990s and 2000s the results didn't matter that much. It was being part of the Wales Away team of supporters which really counted.

Back then we knew we were a poor side and almost took pride in being the underdogs, always second-best. To the tune of 'Those were the days my friend' we would sing 'We'll never qualify, we'll never qualify'. It was true, then. Of course we wanted to win and we would celebrate a goal, usually an individual effort by the odd superstar who happened to be Welsh. But with most of our players being dragged from the lower divisions to play for Wales and managers who couldn't run the proverbial whelk stall, there was never any real prospect of qualification for a major tournament. That aside, it was always great fun. Disappointment wasn't painful in those days. It was normal. We were immune to it. I sometimes wonder if we were all happier then with the 90 minutes of football taking a decidedly back seat to the craic. That's unfair. In recent years we have had results and a three-day party every time Wales play away.

So why did we then, and why do most of us still, do it? Writing about football in South Korea, Devon Rowcliffe says we do it for the same reason everyone does it the world over, 'Regardless of which country you may live in, football's most committed supporters tend to be social outcasts in need of a tribe.' I am not sure about being an outcast but I am certainly part of a tribe. Rowcliffe goes on to say, 'Everyone who watches sport does so as a form of escapism, but the most passionate supporters construct a considerable portion of their identity upon what to most people is merely ephemeral entertainment.'

That 'creation of identity' Devon refers to is particularly important to Wales football fans. The years of failure on the pitch have somehow reflected a wider feeling of political impotence in our everyday lives. We have been marginalised at the very edge of the United Kingdom and basically been told to know our place. The game, and the national team's recent success, allows us to transcend all this, to wave the flag with pride, without requiring consent – on our terms.

Writing in his fanzine *Alternative Wales*, Ryan March says that growing up in a rugby-obsessed community, Welsh football provided him with a 'safe space' where he was surrounded by like-minded people. He says, 'This community had its own culture, its own soundtrack, its own style. It even had its own sense of humour. It was inclusive of gender, race, age, class and even nationality. In my head I thought of us as the "Alternative Wales". Forget rugby, Tom Jones and the south Wales valleys' stereotypes. It's the whole of Wales, not just Cardiff and the Valleys. It's Bala, Newtown, Caernarfon, Denbigh, Aberystwyth, Carmarthen, Monmouth and everywhere else in between, and when we join the national football team, it's truly a community from the whole of Wales.'

Over the years, work colleagues laughed at me taking my family on holiday to Latvia in order to watch a friendly. 'What? You took an eight-year-old out of school to go to Azerbaijan?' In the pub they would ask why I wasn't following a 'decent' team like Liverpool. Ah, South Wales. The biggest suburb Liverpool never knew it had. I think a lot of people pitied me. They certainly thought I was odd. But I had the last laugh. On those summer nights of 2016 in Bordeaux, Lens, Lille, Toulouse, Paris and Lyon (I just love rattling that list off) and yes, right there on the Eisteddfod field in the middle of nowhere, winking at Ifor from Machynlleth, this had been our time. Wales had taken part in a major championship in my lifetime. This was my game, my team, my real and adoptive family, my country. I knew it. Ifor knew it. And d'you know what? That's all that counts.

Epilogue

I GRITTED my teeth as I climbed the carpeted staircase to the Chairman's Lounge at the Cardiff City Stadium. Wales were playing Slovakia in their first qualifying game for Euro 2020. There had been no early pint with the family in Wetherspoons for me this time. My beloved 1976 replica shirt had been replaced by a sober suit and tie. Today, armed with a glossy pass strung around my neck, I was headed for pre-match hospitality.

The wood-panelled room was, as expected, full of old men wearing the same regulation blazers and association ties, and yes they were filling up on the free food and drink before kick-off. It is easy to mock the 'prawn sandwich brigade' but over the years every one of these guys (and just a few women too) had paid their dues to the game. Here were the managers, coaches, referees and secretaries that make football tick. Without them there would be no national game. A decent meal, a few bevvies and a chance to sit in the posh seats was scant reward for the hours they had all put in.

I grabbed a beer and sidled up to a couple of council members. One was an old hand whom I had known for years, but the other, like me, was a comparative newbie to this kind of affair. They were discussing Wales's upcoming away games. We were playing in Croatia and then three days later in Hungary. 'I think we should get four points out of them,' said the older guy. 'Aye, it should be interesting,' said the new recruit. 'But it's wrong isn't it? Making the fans travel to two away games one after the other like that. It's going to cost them a fortune. And then there's the time off work they'll have to take.' The old hand sighed. 'Come on,' he said, 'you're speaking like a supporter now. There are far more important things to think about in football.'

I fear that the governance of the game of football is riddled with this kind of groupthink, where the desire for harmony or conformity in a group can result in irrational or dysfunctional decision-making. It felt to me as if the new kid on the block was being brought into the fold, being told, not too subtly, to leave the supporter in him at the gate. His presence here in the gilded cage of football's movers and shakers meant that he must now take on board more pressing considerations – broadcasting rights, travel plans (the squad's, not the fans', of course) and the demands of UEFA; in summary, what's 'best for the game'.

The denigration of supporters has been a recurring theme in this book. It sometimes feels like contempt and reflects a growing dislocate between those who run the game, especially the professional game, and those who are its true owners, the players and supporters, young and old. For me, the game reflects the society we live in and that society is itself shaped by the economic system in which it operates.

Professional football exemplifies the excesses of neo-liberal economics; ticket prices, players' wages and transfer fees, travel arrangements, television kick-off times, the price of replica shirts, third kits, the cost of your Sky subscription, take your pick. The supposed trickle down of money to the grassroots is actually a trickle up to the top. Ownership and control of the game is in the hands of the few, and it is organised for the benefit of, that's right, those who own and control it. The people paying for it all, you and me, were sidelined long ago. We became infantilised and made helpless as we drifted into a false consciousness that *they* know what's best for the game and what's best for us.

In his misleadingly titled book *How Football Explains the World: An Unlikely Theory of Globalisation*, Franklin Foer describes the power of the game to excite, challenge and change society, for good and for bad. He shows how women in Iran have taken on the theocratic authorities just by attending a football match. He describes the continuing religious and 'national' rivalries in the game across Europe and the cynical selling of Brazil's best players to foreign teams for the short-term gain of the 'top hats' and at considerable cost to the domestic game itself.

Foer also asks why football has never really caught on in the United States. He suggests it is a backlash to the promotion of a 'foreign' and middle-class game, with teams usually based on the eastern and western seaboards. Soccer is perceived as anti-American by the real America of the midwest. Why the title of his book is misleading is because Foer concludes that despite its massive cultural footprint, its truly globalised appeal and reach, football is at the same time reinforcing local identities, inter-club rivalries and in places like Italy and Brazil even local corruptions. It may be a global phenomenon but it does not explain globalisation.

Was I the only one who sighed when the Wrexham Supporters' Trust sold the club to two well-known and seemingly well-meaning American millionaires? Ryan Reynolds and Rob McElhenney are funny guys who have a great track record in Hollywood but what do they know about football? The Swansea City Supporters' Trust also agreed the sale of its club to Americans who had only a limited track record in the game. They cashed in the Swans' best players and it has taken the club years to get back to where they were.

Both supporters' trusts balloted their members before voting for the takeovers. It seems such a pity that even with an educated and willing fanbase, taking back control of the game on a club-by-club basis still seems a distant prospect. I don't have the answers but I do know that every time a community-owned club 'does what it has to do to stay in the game' we lose something valuable.

As it happens I was not the only person dismayed at the sale of Wrexham AFC. Writing in the *SHAG* fanzine, long-standing Red Dragons supporter Ap Dafydd said of the takeover, 'Make no bones about it, we have sold our soul.' He argues that the supporter trust model of ownership is seen by most fans simply as a means to an end. They come together to save the club in a time of crisis, but are really only waiting for a sugar daddy to choose them as their next pet project. 'So many of our fans never bought into the idea of fan ownership. They were waiting to hand over the reins the first chance they had, to chase the soulless dream of the Premier League. There is nothing more wretched, nothing that has sullied the game I love more than the money men, Sky Sports and the bloody Premier League.' But despite feeling compromised, even Ap Dafydd voted for the takeover.

The reality is that football is part of the globalised entertainment network. The only difference is that because of their lifelong commitment and investment, emotionally as well as financially, its consumers can be exploited in much greater levels before they disconnect. Daniel Lambert, who is reinventing the Irish club Bohemian FC as an inner-city community club in Dublin, puts it even more bluntly. He says, 'Football clubs globally have become toys for the mega-rich – taking what were essential parts of towns, cities and people's identities, sense of place and turning them into meaningless businesses with no emotional connection.' I think that's what hurts, knowing that those doing the exploiting, can and do cynically use and abuse supporters because we won't, or in my case cannot, walk away.

Despite all this there is still much good in the game, from bringing communities together and creating friendships to rehabilitating prisoners. So I want to end on an upbeat note. Think for a minute about standing on the touchline as your son or daughter is put through their paces on a rainy Saturday morning. It's wet and miserable but you wouldn't want to be anywhere else, would you? Or there you are screaming for joy as your team scores in added time. Whoever owns your club, however exploitative are the players, their agents and the 'top hats', football still allows you to think you are part of the team. Their success is your success. They give us dreams to dream and they make us believe that we are part of their story. And here's the twist. In fact we are a part of their story, a crucial part, and if it weren't for our support they wouldn't exist. It's we who put them there no matter how big they are.

Acknowledgements

I AM indebted to Lefi Gruffudd and Y Lolfa for their support for my first two books and for allowing me to revisit some chapters from *Kicking off in North Korea* here. An early version of *Doing the 92* was first published on the Football History Boys website.

I would like to thank Jonny Owen for writing the introduction to this book and Geraint Tregaron who has always encouraged me to write and has been steadfast in his support. Thanks also to Alex McDonald for his proofreading.

My love of football has always been informed by the people I stand, and now more often sit, with, to watch games. Thanks then to my intrepid fellow groundhoppers, Kevin Davies and David Collins, for their company all over Europe. Only now can we laugh at how our flags were taken down by teenage ultras at a match in Koblenz. It wasn't funny at the time.

Thanks to Huw Morgan for organising the visit to TeBe in the One Nations, Two Game chapter and to Yvonne Siemon and to Dr Christophe Wagner for their insights into the game in Germany.

Chester has been an honest if unforgiving sub-editor. In the early days of travelling, I would blame his youthful enthusiasm for the need to bunk off school to go to Armenia for a week, or more importantly to Rotherham on a Tuesday night. It was all in the name of a rounded education you understand. Diolch Chester.

Floodlight pictures
(from top left clockwise)

Friedrich-Ludwig-Jahn-Sportpark, BFC Dynamo, Berlin.

Hong Kong FC Stadium, Happy Valley Racecourse, Hong Kong.

Ninian Park, Cardiff City (courtesy of Mark Watkins).

La Linea de la Concepcion, southern Spain (courtesy of David Collins).

Station JNA, Partizan Belgrade (courtesy of Marko Mihaljevic).

BK Frem, Copenhagen.

Aberaman Park, Aberdare Town FC.

Oakwell, Barnsley (courtesy of David Collins).

Hrazdan Central Stadium, Yerevan, Armenia.

Bibliography

Amado J. (2013) *The Violent Land.* New York: Penguin

BBC Sport (2003) *Blatter condemns European clubs.* Online. www.news.bbc.co.uk/sport1/hi/football/africa/3326971.stm

Blum S. (2019) *Why Racism Is on the Rise in Soccer Again.* Online. www.gq.com

Brophy J. (2020) KOREA PATH Meet Han Kwang-Song. Online. www.thesun.co.uk

Burnell N. (2019) *Trailing Clouds of Glory – Welsh football's forgotten heroes of 1976.* Aberystwyth: Y Lolfa

Crolley L and Hand D. (2006) *Football and European identity: historical narratives through the press.* London: Routledge

Demick B. (2005) *Soccer Riot in Tightly Controlled North Korea Surprises Observers.* Online. www.latimes.com

Dymock N (2020) *Wales Supporters Team.* Online. www.walessupporters.co.uk

Feffer J. (2017) *Aftershock – A Journey into Eastern Europe's Broken Dreams.* London: Zed Books

Foer F. (2004) *How Football Explains The World: An Unlikely Theory of Globalisation.* London: Harper Collins

Grundy J. (2019) *90 Minutes of Freedom.* Cardiff: Self-published

Hartley T. (ed.) (2016) *Merci France.* Aberystwyth: Y Lolfa

Hartley T. (2016) *Kicking off in North Korea – Football and Friendship in Foreign Lands.* Aberystwyth: Y Lolfa

Johnes M. (2000) *Eighty Minute Patriots? National Identity and Sport in Modern Wales.* The International Journal of the History of Sport, Vol.17, No.4. London: Frank Cass

Johnes M. (2012) *Why a football TeamGB is a threat to the independence of the 'home nations.'* Online. www.martinjohnes.com/2012/07/21/

Lee C. (2021) *Political Football: CE Júpiter.* Outside Write. Online. www.outsidewrite.co.uk

Linder A. (2019) *Musicians in gas masks perform orchestra version of Hong Kong's 'new national anthem.'* Shanghaiist. Online. www.shanghaiist.com/2019/09/12/

McAllister L. (2019*) If there is a women's football Team GB at the Tokyo Olympics, ignoring it might be the best response.* Western Mail. 22 June 2019

McDougall A. (2019) *The People's Game.* Cambridge: Cambridge University Press

Mills R. (2013) *Fighters, footballers and nation builders: wartime football in the Serb-held territories of the former Yugoslavia, 1991–1996.* Taylor and Francis. Online. www.tandfonline.com/

Radio GDR (2019) *East German Football – The People's Game:Football, State and Society in East Germany.* Online. www.radiogdr.com/east-german-football/

Rowcliffe D. (2020) *Who ate all the squid?* Worthing: Pitch Publishing

Singleton C. et al (2020) *As football returns in empty stadiums, four graphs show how home advantage disappears.* Online. www.theconversation.com/

Stüve C. (2020) *German reunification: What happened to East Germany's top football clubs?* Online. www.dw.com

Todorov B. and Shentov O. (ed.) (2015) *Radicalisation in Bulgaria: Threats and Trends.* Centre for the Study of Democracy. Bulgaria. Online. www.http://old.csd.bg/artShowbg.php?id=17707

Various (2019) *Members Stories.* Clapton CFC. Online. www.claptoncfc.co.uk/members-stories/

Westby M. (2017) *A History of Sheffield Football 1857–1889: Speed, Science and Bottom.* Sheffield: England's Oldest Football Clubs

Wright G. (2019) *Bulgarian football and its problem with racism.* Online. www.bbc.co.uk/news/world-europe-50060759